A Study of Moses Waddel, 1770-1840,

As

Teacher and Puritan

James Lewis MacLeod F.S.A. (Scot.)

Copyright 1995
By: James Lewis MacLeod

All rights reserved. No part of this publication may be reproduced, stored in a retrieval system, transmitted in any form, posted on to the web in any form or by any means without the prior written permission of the publisher.

This book was printed by:

www.southernhistoricalpress.com
or
**SOUTHERN HISTORICAL PRESS, Inc.
PO BOX 1267
375 West Broad Street
Greenville, SC   29601**
southernhistoricalpress@gmail.com

ISBN #0-89308-546-4

Library Congress Catalog Number: 84-52026

Printed in the United States of America

for:

Sara Macaulay McLeod

AUTHOR

A Presbyterian minister's son, the author was sent to "prep" for college at the Darlington School, Rome, Georgia, then received his B.A. degree from a center of Southern history, Washington and Lee University. A history major, the author was a student under the historian Arnold J. Toynbee, then a visiting professor at Washington and Lee. MacLeod was also taught by the social historian, James G. Leyburn, author of The Scotch-Irish: A Social History and Dean at Washington and Lee.

In graduate work MacLeod received a Master of Arts in Teaching at Emory University, Atlanta, an Educational Specialist's Degree in School Administration, and his Doctorate in Secondary Education from Mississippi State University. His doctoral dissertation researched early American education in Charleston, South Carolina. MacLeod studied on a postgraduate basis at schools in France and Germany. Interested in theology, he attended Princeton Theological Seminary, Princeton, New Jersey, and the Candler School of Theology, Emory University, where he received another Master's degree in theology and religion.

MacLeod's practical experience in education includes college teaching, school administration and three times a "Star" teacher in Georgia secondary schools. He is certified in teaching "gifted" students. In 1980 the author was chosen by the U.S. "Fulbright" Board to study at Jadavapur University in Calcutta, India. He was chosen in 1984 by the "Fulbright" Teacher Exchange to teach in Great Britain.

The author's practical experience, awareness of educational methods, research in early American education, familiarity with the social history of the Scotch-Irish, and his theological and religious learning have made him uniquely skilled to assess the great, perhaps, greatest educator, the South has ever known, Moses Waddel.

MacLeod's style of writing is intentionally lucid, a circumstance not always found in works of historical and particularly educational scholarship. The author attributes much of this absence of buzz words and scholarly jargon, commonly known as "educationese," to his early training in writing by a literary friend, Georgia author, Flannery O'Connor. Her emphases were for him studiously to avoid jargon as well that tiresome piety that too often has marred studies of prominent Southern historical personages of this era. MacLeod recalls her saying, "you don't have to write like Henry James to be complex," and her sly observation, "A Ph.D. affects some sholars like religion affects other folks. They think they've got to speak in the unknown tongue to prove they've really got it."

Dr. MacLeod observes, "If I wrote in the scholarly educational jargon about Waddel's school, I would have to write: "The emphasis in this educational unit was time on task. The result was successful engaged learning." Well, of course, that's nonsense. Translated into English it means Waddel's school meant hard work and the students learned a lot. (In educational scholarly jargon a school is called an educational unit, getting students to work is time on task, and successful engaged learning means somebody learned something.)

Dr. MacLeod was one of Flannery O'Connor's pallbearers. He comments, "From her I learned a scholarly book is never to read like a government pamphlet. That's too easy a way out. The difficulty seems to be that while a scholar may do good research, he or she may often be too insecure, untrained, or even academically frightened to say it in lucid English, something people can understand. A reformation is needed in writing English, not only in the schools, but in the professional educational circles that run them. This book is a trail blazer and something of a pioneer in that aspect."

MacLeod is descended from a family who sent their sons to Waddel, the Griers, a prominent pioneer Scotch-Irish family that produced the Rev. Isaac Grier, first Presbyterian minister born in Georgia, a U.S. Supreme Court Judge, several college presidents, Georgia's Alexander Stephens, Vice-President of the Confederacy, and Robert Grier, founder of Grier's "Almanac," referred to as a Bible for the Southern ante-bellum farmer. It was the death of Robert Grier, the "Almanacer" that inspired his nephew, Alexander Stephens, to introduce as a U.S. Congressman the bill that founded the National Weather Bureau. Both the Rev. Isaac Grier and Alexander Stephens went to school to Waddel.

In December 1984 MacLeod was elected a Fellow of the Society of Antiquaries of Scotland in Edinburgh.

TABLE OF CONTENTS

PREFACE

I.	OLD MOSES.	1
II.	AN AMERICAN ETON	5
III.	FRANKLIN COLLEGE	7
IV.	THE SCOTCH-IRISH	10
V.	BORN	15
VI.	BORN AGAIN	19
VII.	HAMPDEN-SYDNEY	23
VIII.	THE LOW COUNTRY.	27
IX.	CARMEL	32
X.	MARRIAGE	36
XI.	WILLINGTON	41
XII.	FREEDOM AND JUSTICE FOR ALL.	46
XIII.	TEACHER.	50
XIV.	CURRICULUM	55
XV.	LEADERS FROM THE WOODS	61
XVI.	CROMWELL OF THE CLASSROOM.	65
XVII.	COMMENCEMENT AND COLLEGE	70
XVIII.	DECISIONS, DECISIONS	75
XIX.	THE UNIVERSITY OF GEORGIA.	81
XX.	MINISTER	92
XXI.	REVIVALISM AND THE COLLAPSE OF THE COVENANT.	97
XXII.	THE DIVINE VISITATION.	103
XXIII.	THE CALVINIST PARADOX.	108
XXIV.	PLANTATION LIFE.	111
XXV.	DANGERS AND DEPTHS	117

XXVI.	EVALUATION	120
XXVII.	ALUMNI FOREWORD.	125
XXVIII.	FIFTY WADDEL ACADEMY ALUMNI (Biographies). .	127
XXXIX.	FORTY WADDEL UNIVERSITY OF GEORGIA ALUMNI. .	137
	FOOTNOTES.	142
	BIBLIOGRAPHY	172

PREFACE

Thanks are due to Dr. Walter Sistrunk, Community College Department, Mississippi State University: Dr. Glover Moore, Professor of Southern History and author of The Kentucky Compromise; the late Dr. Neill W. Macaulay, Columbia, South Carolina, for invaluable assistance in locating sources; Mrs. Martha Bailey Burns, Secretary of the Huguenot Society of South Carolina at Charleston for her help and research on her family, the Legares, as well as other Huguenot history. Thanks are also due to Ms. Betty Gardiner, research librarian, Dr. H. Elizabeth King, Chief Psychologist, Emory University, for review and consultation on Waddel's nervous collapses; Dr. Charles Davis of Georgia Southern College for his editor's skill, and the library and staff of the South Caroliniana Library, University of South Carolina at Columbia; the library staff of the University of North Carolina at Chapel Hill; and historian Dixon Hollingsworth of Sylvania, Georgia, for good advice.

"This day I am to go to Willington; with joy and fear I view the vast design."

                James Louis Petigru to his diary, October 14, 1804.

"This day, my dear Carey, marks an important epoch in my life...58 years ago I was well received into the school at Willington...where a Latin grammar, as a substitute for the plough, was placed in my hands."

                James Louis Petigru in a letter to his daughter, dated October 14, 1862.

OLD MOSES

The fact that it does not take a great mind to be a great teacher ought to be a comfort to many presently teaching. Moses Waddel, one of the most successful of American teachers, the South's greatest educator, illustrates this. His mind was conventional and his thinking largely unoriginal. His morality was backward even for his time (early nineteenth century) and creed (Calvinism). Although his only written work, Memoirs Of The Life of Miss Caroline Elizabeth Smelt, is as nauseating as its name, so completely did he express the sentiments of his time that the book went through five depressing editions and won the applause of the pious semi-literate.[1] One cannot believe that his diary, the product of a mind that was like a Sunday School lesson, was that of a great teacher. He believed completely in his Calvinistic creed, so deeply perhaps that there was, as there was in Stonewall Jackson, a streak of poetry in this man whenever he thought fervently on trumpets sounding, the dead rising, and hovering angels, like gulls, circling the air above the church which St. Augustine compared to a ship.

Perhaps this belief in some way sustained him, because he won the race, tortoise-like, through the steady application of evangelical virtues. Governor George Gilmer of Georgia, one of his students, said he was "a most admirable example of the superiority of a strong sense of duty and untiring industry in the employments of life, over genius and accomplishments."[2] Some teachers may be heard to say that they would prefer a serious and steady student to an unsteady, brilliant one. The career of Waddel suggests that this attitude may not be so philistine as it sounds. The slow and pious tortoise may surpass the more sophisticated hare--not always perhaps, but at least sometimes. Dr. Waddel was a tortoise, awkward, bizarre, sometimes downright ugly, yet always puritanically enduring and mystically carrying on in his church dome shell. For there can be absolutely, as far as classification, no question Dr. "Waddle" (for this was the way he pronounced "Waddel") belonged to the tortoises of this life. There is no doubt "the famous Dr. Waddel" was also genuinely pious and believed himself to be an elect and predestined tortoise. This knowledge kept him, as the family joked, "waddling along."

He was no hypocrite. A recurring theme in his sermons was the necessity of going into the closet to meet God alone,[3] thereby avoiding pretentious religious show, lest faith become a false and public thing. He himself spent hours in private prayer over his life, his school, and his students, morbidly enjoying the agonies of a Calvinistic conscience. He viewed his students' learning as other ministers viewed their souls, as his dreadful and awesome responsibility before God. He gave each student's learning careful evangelical analysis, as if a soul were at stake, which in a way it was. Because he considered that so much was involved, he was not afraid to innovate in teaching techniques, with results that were amazing. Furthermore, Old Moses used peer pressure and what might be called today "group dynamics" quite cleverly. He had a very realistic understanding of the use of discipline and the possibilities of structuring power. He also had the traditional Calvinistic "iron will," that suspect term seemingly always draped around early Calvinists.

A good proof of his iron will was that he performed all this in the deep South, in Georgia and South Carolina, in oppressive heat and under crude conditions. The antebellum black people and many white ones must have found his dazzling display of Presbyterian industry and virtues quite mad, placing him in the same category that Noel Coward had in mind a century later when he described the "mad dogs and Englishmen" who went out in the noonday sun as the natives took siestas. But at the same time, they knew better than to try to deter him. It is seldom wise to accord such treatment to people who believe themselves elected by God. Aflame with irritation, part of the time he was capable of the unexpected, an exciting quality that boys particularly like and which is demonstrated in an unforgettable vignette of his flaring temper.

Dr. Waddel, whip in hand, was chasing a disobedient boy across a field, with both Sam, the offender, and Waddel going faster and faster as delighted boys came from everywhere to watch, whistle and jeer: "Look at Old Moses go! He is catching up!" Sam, hoping to escape, jumped a hedge, but as he went over the hedge, Waddel, presented with a perfect target, gave Sam a swipe that made him go higher than either Sam or any of the onlookers thought possible.[4] His work accomplished, Waddel went back to his office as adolescent watchers laughed till their sides hurt and a chastened Sam dusted himself off on the other side. Although the incident may be a bit shocking to moderns, something mysteriously psychological happened. The story of the chase was to be told over and over by men who would always think of themselves as Old Moses' boys. (Even though James Louis Petigru felt that as a boy he had been unjustly punished by Old Moses, Petigru, a middle-aged lawyer, was overcome with tears when he heard of Waddel's death.) Anna Freud has said that in successful teaching the teacher becomes the student's super ego. In this way can be understood the remark of A. B. Longstreet, author of <u>Georgia Scenes</u> and ante-bellum president of several universities, that Waddel brought about those changes in Longstreet's character that made him successful. By those or any terms, Waddel was a successful teacher.

Waddel's Academy, in fact, was the most successful in the Old South. Because of the unusual number of statesmen and luminaries it turned out, the school was referred to as the "American Eton," although "Southern Eton" might have been a more fitting description. Besides a host of physicians, lawyers, and ministers, the doctor's tutelage produced eminent statesmen, teachers, and writers. There were William H. Crawford, Madison's Secretary of the Treasury, Hugh S. Legare, editor of the <u>Southern Review</u>; Governor George McDuffie of South Carolina, Governor Gilmer of Georgia, A. B. Longstreet, the president of two universities, and John C. Calhoun.

Nor were Dr. Waddel's alumni in one mould made. They ranged from John C. Calhoun, the father of secession, to testy, eccentric James Louis Petigru of Charleston, a witty lawyer who opposed secession to the end and facetiously referred to secessionists as lunatics. Nor did these students succumb to Waddel's religious views. John C. Calhoun remained a free thinker. A. B. Longstreet, of a more religious temperament, examined his teacher's Presbyterianism carefully and became a Methodist.

It was in formulating lifelong values, inspiring students to realize their potential, teaching them enjoyment of the classical writers, awakening their ambitions and preparing them thoroughly for college that the Academy excelled. In old-fashioned terms it was said that Waddel "disciplined the mind." He ran a very competent prep school that introduced, for the most part, raw country boys to the life of the mind, taught them Calvinistic self-discipline, and schooled them well in the texts of the time. Many of them internalized his discipline and went off to colleges to become well-known. They were to become gentlemen of the Old South, a professional elite, part of an "old boy network" of 4,000 alumni.[5]

Wadel's Academies appealed to the Southern elite. Such proud aristocrats as the Telfairs of Savannah, the Noble Wimberley Joneses of "Wormsloe" plantation in Georgia, the Legares of Charleston, and the Taylors, the first family of Columbia, South Carolina, sent their sons to Waddel. Although begun to serve primarily the backwoods Scotch-Irish, it also served the socially elite.

Dr. Waddel's Academy was called an Eton, of course, because it produced so many leaders. But it was actually Dr. Thomas Arnold of Rugby that Dr. Waddel resembled. In fact, W. J. Grayson in his biography of James Louis Petigru even called Waddel the "Carolina Dr. Arnold."[6] However, such a characterization is misleading; Waddel was a predecessor of Thomas Arnold, not an imitator. After all, when Waddel set up the school at Willington in 1804, Arnold was nine years old. To be sure, there was in both preachers the same earnest and energetic faith, the same evangelical bent, the desire to uplift, a similar utilization of peer group pressure towards new ends, the same belief in punishment as an answer, the same attention to the morals, habits, and manners of the students. There was also the same classical education.

Education consists of two parts: socialization and the quite different ability to think and reason. There was in the schools of both men a heavy emphasis on socialization because both Waddel and Arnold wished to produce Christian gentlemen. If the boys learned morality from the headmasters, presumably they learned the ability to think from their classical curriculum where they associated and became familiar with the greatest minds of the past. Certainly John C. Calhoun cannot be understood apart from a familiarity with the logic of Aristotle. George McDuffie's prose style was pre-Ciceronian. James Louis Petigru's emphasis on the law was a clear reflection of the Roman mind. In an elaborate era Hugh Legare's prose style reflected a familiarity with Attic simplicity. These gentlemen were schooled in the tradition of a classical education, the proper schooling for a gentleman of that period. Today classical education is confined largely to the few bored students in high school Latin. In the Southeast from 1804 to 1819, the classics were in the hands of Dr. Moses Waddel, whom Calhoun called "the father of classical education in the upper country." However, one has the feeling that Old Moses could have handled any school curriculum, any system of formal schooling, at his log cabin academy at Willington, South Carolina.

In 1819 this Cromwell of the classroom again demonstrated his abilities when he became the fifth President of a failing University of Georgia. When he arrived Georgia was down to its name, seven students, and practically empty buildings.[7] In three years the enrollment was 120 students, and two new buildings were under construction. The "famous Dr. Waddel" saved the day--and, quite literally, the college. Then in 1829 he returned to his academy at Willington to do further pioneer work in democratic education in America. Having before organized a student government with a system of trials by peer groups for student offenses, on his return he added to this system by writing a high school code of laws. His school was often called a "rural republic."

As if an innovative and remarkable career in schooling were not enough, he maintained an enormous involvement in church work. In his function as minister he was unceasing: preaching countless sermons, conducting prayer meetings, addressing Bible societies, and doing good deeds.

He accomplished all this even though he was never really a physically well person. His was the soul of iron of a Scotch-Irish Presbyterian that largely made him what he was: sometimes comic, even macabre, and dogmatic, but also determined, disciplined, and achieving. Hot tempered, irritable, at times even ungracious, he may surely have been, but he had character and could teach students how to apply it to books and life.

AN AMERICAN ETON

W. J. Grayson was not engaging in an exalted flight of rhetoric when he compared what Willington was in South Carolina to what Eton was to England, the principal training ground for leadership. Students Waddel trained at Willington headed for leadership positions in South Carolina like racehorses trained for the finish line. From 1820 to 1860 Waddel's students gave a dazzling display.

Four elected governors of South Carolina in a row had gone to school to Waddel.[1] All the speakers of the South Caroline House of Representatives from 1833 to 1847 were Waddel students.[2] Three United States Senators trained by Waddel went to Washington from 1840 to 1850.[3] Thirteen United States Representatives from South Carolina went to Washington between 1820 and 1860.[4] Three "Law" judgeships in succession were filled by Willington students.[5] One Waddel-trained Attorney General of South Carolina replaced another.[6] In 1850 the Judge of the Court of Equity as well as the U.S. District Attorney for South Carolina had gone to Willington.[7] The President of the Bank of South Carolina was an alumnus,[8] as were the Presidents of the Charlotte and South Carolina Railroad and the Savannah Valley Railroad.[9] In 1857 the mayors of the rival towns of Charleston and Savannah were both Waddel-schooled.[10] The Chancellor of South Carolina[11] was a faithful member of the swelling alumni chorus singing Waddel's praises that was led by the President of the University of South Carolina.[12]

In antebellum South Carolina it seemed as if the whole world, or everyone who mattered, had gone to Willington. Dr. Waddel was unofficial headmaster to the state. He furnished more leadership to South Carolina than any man but John C. Calhoun and, since he taught Calhoun too, that hardly counted. The cliché is that the hand that rocks the cradle rules the world. In Dr. Waddel's case the hand that held the paddle ruled the state.

The students of the grimly determined Puritan did not do badly in Georgia either. Two United States Senators, five members of the U.S. House of Representatives, and three governors went to school to him.[13] Even in "faraway" Alabama a governor, a United States Senator, a Chief Justice of the Alabama Supreme Court, one Chancellor, and one member of the United States House of Representatives were schooled under Waddel.[14] An ordinary academy in the South would have been glad to claim the Alabama alumni alone and call fame quits.

On a more national level Waddel' claimed nine governors,[15] three U.S. Secretaries of War,[16] two Secretaries of State,[17] one Secretary of the Treasury,[18] and a Vice President of the United States.[19] He taught two antebellum war heroes,[20] and in Civil War five members of the Confederate

Congress, one Confederate governor and one Confederate Brigadier-general had been schooled by him.[21] There also came from his academies a dozen authors or editors of newspapers[22] and five college presidents.[23]

Although it would be ridiculous to assume that Waddel's teaching by itself made his students what they were, it would be equally ridiculous to disregard him or his schools as a factor. His schooling represented one variable that may or may not have been important according to each case. Full judgement of this simply cannot be known.

The case of Governor Patrick Noble of South Carolina shows, if any does, the effects of Waddel's schooling. Chancellor Alexander Bowie of Alabama said of Noble that he was amiable but his mind had no brilliant parts. Although he was well-read and had a retentive memory,[24] he had little imagination. However, he had firmness of purpose proceeding from a high sense of duty.[25] In his sense of moral duty and the ability to keep working toward a purpose may be seen the strong hand of Waddel, of whom such characteristics were trademarks. The biographer of Dr. James Proctor Screven said that he was "willing to put in superhuman labor to achieve his purpose'[26]--again the stamp of Waddel: high morality and hard work. Indeed very few of Waddel's students were ever said to be brilliant. The ones who rose to fame or prominence were striking, not in their intellect, but in being well-schooled, hard-working, and highly moral.

To be sure, Waddel students were often well-placed enough in family and wealth and college degrees to have entrée, but entrée in itself is no good without the capability to produce after being introduced. And indeed after a while the fact of having been a student at Willington was an introduction in itself. After more time had passed, the fact of having a father, grandfather, or uncle who had gone to Willington or studied under Dr. Waddel was seen as proof of a family of high degree in the South, knowing the "right" people.

Walt Whitman said, "Political democracy, as it exists and practically works in America, with all its threatening evils, supplies a training school for making first class men." This is what Waddel's "Christian" schools were: training schools for making first class men. The many first class men produced by them formed a galaxy around Waddel. The career of Waddel does make it seem as if a great teacher is a sun whose teaching shoots off stars. Or, perhaps, great teaching is a magnetic force pulling others into orbit. The force remains as mysterious today as it did in Waddel's time. But Presbyterian Waddel did produce an elect, a spiritual elite, a galaxy of leaders. His teaching may be said to be a comet that left a trail of stars through the paths it cut.

FRANKLIN COLLEGE

(The University of Georgia)

Waddel did not use the same educational methods and techniques at Franklin College as he did at Willington, but the college turned out many distinguished students under his supervision. It should be remembered that the college was small, smaller actually than Willington in the latter's best years, and had a larger staff. Personal and even intimate supervision was possible and was given. The image of Dr. Waddel scanning the horizon with his spyglass is a very real reminder of Waddel's intimate and detailed knowledge of campus life.

The mark of the Waddel student can be seen in the description of Dr. Paul Eve, who was the first American surgeon to do a hysterectomy and was in 1857-58 President of the American Medical Association. Eve is said to have been tone deaf and near-sighted but overcame these handicaps through hard work and "methodical" industry. It was the same sort of description that characterized the "almost German" thoroughness of the writings of Hugh Swinton Legare, the extraordinary work ability of James P. Screven, and the plodding industry of Governor Patrick Noble. It was also characteristic of Waddel himself, as Governor George Gilmer pointed out.

Although Willington and the early academies left no catalogues and yearly student listings, the University of Georgia did. The list of those matriculating prior to 1821, however, has been lost, and even the lists that are extant are not complete. For example, Francis W. Pickens, Governor of South Carolina, 1860-62, who attended the University of Georgia before transferring to the University of South Carolina and dropping out in 1827 in his senior year, is not mentioned. Therefore, of course, not all the students who either graduated or matriculated under Dr. Waddel are known.

Records reveal that in ten years at the University of Georgia Waddel schooled one governor of Georgia,[1] one U.S. Senator from Georgia,[2] and eleven U.S. Congressmen from Georgia.[3] In addition his college students included one governor of South Carolina,[4] two U.S. congressmen from Alabama,[5] thirteen judges of various degrees,[6] three college presidents,[7] six newspaper editors or authors,[8] one Supreme Court Justice,[9] one minister to Russia,[10] one president of the American Medical Association,[11] an Anglican bishop,[12] a Methodist bishop,[13] 35 clergymen,[14] and one poet.[15]

Furthermore, he schooled at the University of Georgia the Vice-President of the Confederacy,[16] the Secretary of

State of the Confederacy,[17] the Assistant Secretary of War of the Confederacy,[18] one Confederate congressman,[19] one Confederate Brigadier-general,[20] and a congressman of the Republic of Texas.[21] (He even produced a "traitor": A Union Brigadier-general.[22])

If alumni of Willington and Waddel's other academies are totalled with the University of Georgia to make a complete Waddel alumni list, then the students whom Waddel schooled make a more than formidable display. He schooled two Vice-Presidents,[23] three Secretaries of State,[24] three Secretaries of War,[25] one Assistant Secretary of War,[26] one U.S. Attorney-general,[27] ministers to France, Spain and Russia,[28] one U.S. Supreme Court Justice,[29] eleven governors,[30] seven U.S. Senators,[31] thirty-two members of the U.S. House of Representatives,[32] twenty-two judges,[33] eight college presidents,[34] seventeen editors of newspapers or authors,[35] five members of the Confederate Congress,[36] two bishops,[37] three Brigadier-generals,[38] and possibly to represent those being led by the above, one authentic Christian martyr.[39]

The fact that he trained some of the most profound and complex minds of the Old South cannot go unnoticed: John C. Calhoun, Alexander Stephens, Hugh Swinton Legare, James Louis Petigru, A. B. Longstreet, Justice Campbell, and the surgeon Dr. Eve.

Since so many leaders of the Old South shared the experience of Dr. Waddel, any study of him helps us to understand them as well as the Old South. And since the personality of great educators is as much a part of their teaching as any formal school curriculum, the personality of Waddel is of definite historical importance. The leaders of Dixie recalled Waddel the man who was a preacher as well as teacher.

Waddel the personality was a composite of teacher and puritan preacher just as the great Dr. Thomas Arnold of Rugby was. It is as impossible to get a full picutre of Dr. Waddel without his Scotch-Irish puritanism as Dr. Arnold without his Church of England puritanism. It would be as unthinkable to leave out Waddel's religion as to leave out Arnold's. Their religion made the men.

Their religion, Calvinism, had a way of stretching its serious believers to the furthest limits of their abilities thereby making significant achievers out of unusually intelligent or gifted people through the application of its stern intellectual discipline, its agonizing conscientiousness and its Sovereign-God mysticism. Waddel is to be evaluated not as a man born great but as a significant achiever motivated by Calvinism.

The good Calvinist life was to be a fugue elaborating on the theme that the main aim of humanity was to glorify

God in every respect of life as well as enjoy Him forever. Yet, the fact remains, however high, spiritual and moral the tone was to be set, whenever the gut strings of the violin or any other instrument are pulled tight, there are going to be some occasional squeaks and wry noises. Waddel's religion had its squeaks and sour notes. Sometimes it looked as if Christianity were a piano, he played it with his elbows.

The religious impulse brings the moral and spiritual tensions of the individual together to produce an effort that demands an aesthetic judgment. Michelangelo lamented of his day that people saw every kind of beauty but the beauty of holiness. Waddel did not offer so much of the beauty of holiness as the grandeur of holiness and the capability of those motivated by faith. Waddel offers a more modern religious music, certainly not harmony, for some passages of his religious pilgrimage are jarring and atonal, but there is a truth being worked out of the whole. There is a vision to it.

Waddel also felt his religion gave him inner resources to defeat the mental illness that shadowed him all his life. Waddel was a very modern here in that he fought mental illness. Often overwhelmed by life and submerged by its expectations, not knowing what to do, he had nervous breakdowns that lasted for months. He simply would not give up to his darker side. He probably felt it was not his predestination to give up. This quality of determination was said to be Scotch-Irish. They were a people known for not giving up. Waddel was Scotch-Irish through and through.

THE SCOTCH-IRISH

"I am born," begins David Copperfield. For an understanding of Moses Waddel the story should begin, "I am born Scotch-Irish." It is vital to the understanding of Moses Waddel to first understand something of his people, the Scotch-Irish. It would be as useless to explain him apart from this society as to explain a wave apart from its sea. He was so completely their product that Waddel's career in one sense was simply a high-water mark of their cultural values and their views. Scotch-Irish was the term for Scots families who had settled in the Ulster Plantations of Ireland for several generations before finally arriving in America. James G. Leyburn in his social history, The Scotch-Irish, asserts there was not too much Irish blood in these people.[1]

The question of what to do with Catholic Ireland had been an ever-present irritation to the Anglican English since the time of Queen Elizabeth I. Ireland was too close to England to be free and too nationalistic and Catholic in her attitude to be a comfortable province. This was not so with Scotland, a small and misty land, touching England to the north. Its conversion to Presbyterianism in the 16th century under the intrepid preacher, John Knox, had given mildly Protestant England a fiercely Protestant northern neighbor. Cromwell called the Scottish reformation "God's crowning mercy."

Since Ireland would not convert, the sensible thing was to ship the converted to Ireland, thereby gaining some Protestant beachhead on the island. Ulster land was purchased and set aside with the stipulation that the land would be settled by British Protestants.

Naturally few Englishmen would go to Ireland, but the poor, thrifty Scots, drawn by cheap land, emigrated there in large numbers, accompanied by ministers from the Kirk of Scotland (Presbyterian). Once there, they lived away from Scotland for generations, had experiences all their own, and evolved a society all their own. Their unique experiences and relative isolation made them into a subculture that was quite distinct.[2]

When for a variety of reasons these people migrated to America in the 18th century, they did not happily join the melting pot. For the most part they moved into the unsettled wilderness behind previously settled coastal areas of Eastern America. In the hills, plateaus, and valleys of a Piedmont area reaching from Pennsylvania to Georgia they set up their own rural communities, the social center of which was the church and usually an accompanying academy run by the same minister. Some of their more grim Calvinistic aspects were unattractive, but no more repugnant than those of early New Englanders, whom the upcountry settlers resembled in many ways.

When the Scotch-Irish Calvinists came into the South, they found some values and attitudes very different from their own--and not always better. Their insistence on education is an improvement over the attitude of the Royal Governor of a self-satisfied Virginia, Sir William Berkeley, who remarked in the 1660's, "Thank God there are no free schools nor printing...for learning has brought disobedience and heresy...and printing has divulged them both." Even around one hundred years later a South Carolina journalist worried that if a state college was allowed to be established, education would become too "cheap and common," and what was worse, "every man would be for giving his son an education."

The Calvinistic Scotch-Irish, by contrast, wished every man to read the Bible, and upon reaching the South, they set to work. Virginius Dabney in *Liberalism in the South* noted: "Standing, as they did for a highly trained ministry and the democratization of the educational processes, the Presbyterians were the greatest single force for the educational progress in the Southern states during the late eighteenth and early nineteenth centuries."[3]

The Presbyterians achieved much of this educational progress through academies, comparatively inexpensive middle class private schools--vital institutions at a time when there was no widespread free public education. Many of the academies, which were often crudely constructed buildings serving frontier and rural areas, were run by Presbyterian ministers in the shadow of their churches, thus following the urgent advice of John Knox to the Kirk of Scotland, to have a school alongside the church. Although some of these academies later became colleges and universities, most vanished with the coming of the free public schools before the beginning of the twentieth century. But for a while these academies were the bulwark of middle class education, particularly in the South. In 1850 Virginia had 317 academies, North Carolina 272, Georgia 219 and South Carolina 202.[4]

As well as aiding education, the Scotch-Irish taught in the South the Calvinistic emphasis on work and industriousness. The concepts that an occupation is a "calling," that God is glorified through work, and that there is sacred dignity to labor were much needed in a society that was degraded for years by a system of slavery and caste, which demeaned not only labor but the laborer. The Scotch-Irish also brought their predisposition to revolution, which they called vaguely "Whiggery." The Reverend John Harris of South Carolina, a colonial Presbyterian, boasted there was no man in his Scotch-Irish congregation who was not a Whig.[5] The

Scotch-Irish played so large a part in the American Revolution that it is reasonable to question whether it would have succeeded without them. Even their Presbyterian church government was a training ground for participatory democracy. What the Scotch-Irish did not bring with them was attractiveness of personality. One man wrote that "The Scotch-Irish are the most inflexible of people in the world when in the right; and the most vexatiously pig headed and mulish when wrong."[6]

The Scotch-Irish heroes were the statesmen, the minister, and the school teacher, in that order. Their Presbyterian system of government was a complex system of semi-democratic checks and balances that gave them invaluable training in government and made them clever at organization. They were devoted to the Church of Scotland. They believed fervently in schooling and valued academic intelligence--with certain limits. Furthermore, they had characteristics that made them influential beyond their actual numbers. Their thrift enabled them to accumulate the capital needed for economic growth. A hardy people who could seemingly thrive under any conditions, they believed that God had elected them not to gratify them but to bring them a hard time and stiffen their moral fiber. They were eminently fitted for pioneering.

On the other hand, they were rigid and narrow, and their idea of sin often led them to meddle in relatively minor matters of taste. They believed card playing, theater going, dancing, novels, cursing, and adultery were evil--and not necessarily in that order. Especially obsessed with Sabbath-keeping, they remembered the Sabbath day and kept it boring. The last straw was that they seemed to be blind and deaf to the fine arts. Their early hymn-singing without instruments was called the "Presbyterian whine." The interiors of their churches were totally unadorned lecture halls where out of front center arose an equally unadorned pulpit, behind which the ministers stood and bewailed the sins of Israel in sermons at least one hour long.

The Scotch-Irish, essentially pragmatic, did whatever had to be done to thrive or survive. Today that may strike us as callous and insensitive, but to them it was pioneer common sense. For example, the Morrison family, the Scotch-Irish founders of Davidson College in North Carolina, used to joke that Old Jim, the original ancestor in America of a long line of teachers and ministers, killed more red liquor and more red "injuns" than any other man in Pennsylvania.

Moses Waddel was the complete Scotch-Irishman, a living compendium of their beliefs, prejudices, abilities,

and narrow moral views. He does not seem to have ever
questioned his Scotch-Irish society's assumptions, but
made them his own with little doubting. Although he
rose to greatness by inventing new techniques, these
were designed only to further the old conventional
Scotch-Irish value of education. Old Moses fit all
the cultural patterns of Scotch-Irish society--first
a schoolmaster, later the main Scotch-Irish ideal of
a hero, a minister.[7] He accepted prescribed limits for
the use of his intelligence, i.e., Presbyterian creeds
and prevailing social customs, and was determined to
prove his election through respectability and prosperity.
He was helped in achieving the latter by his thrift,
a typical characteristic of his people. (It was said
that a Scotch-Irish man was one who kept the Ten
Commandments and everything else he could get his hands
on.[8]) Thrift at least helps to explain how Waddel,
born poor, died a plantation owner and a slaveholder.
He was clever at institutional government; perhaps the
cleverest thing he ever did was to involve his students
in the school organization. Overall, he had strong
personal integrity that was seen as "character."

But--typically--he was also narrow and moralistic.
He was against an unlimited list of so-called sins,
including dancing, and diligently spanked them out of
his boys. He made Sunday a gray day. He was aesthetically blind. He was a determined, pragmatic, insensitive, aesthetically deficient, honest, clever, learned,
diligent, thrifty, hardworking, dedicated narrow-minded
Calvinist. In the good and in the bad, the famous
"Dr. Waddle" was Scotch-Irish through and through.

Even his distrust of the Anglican church was due
to his Scotch-Irish background. Parliament had passed
ecclesiastical laws for Ireland that disenfranchised
the Presbyterian clergy and forced taxation on the
Scotch-Irish to support the Anglican clergy. Under-
standably these people came to America with no love of
Anglicanism. Then in the Southern states of America
the Scotch-Irish found the Anglican Church established
by law. Each state had its own peculiar irritations
to which the Presbyterians were subject: in colonial
South Carolina there were the "Acts of Conformity";
a marriage service by a dissenting, i.e., non-Anglican,
clergyman was not valid until 1766 in North Carolina
and until 1781 in Virginia. In Virginia state taxes
for the Anglican Church did not cease until 1799, and
the glebe lands were not sold until 1802. Even in
late-founded Georgia there was a tax in colonial times
for the support of the established Anglican Church.
So much resentment did this cause among the Calvinistic
Scotch-Irish that when William Tennent, a Presbyterian
minister of Charleston, was to explain the Revolution
to backcountry people, he used the disestablishment
of Anglicanism as a reason to revolt. Getting rid of
the Anglican establishment was certainly one of the

reasons the Scotch-Irish Presbyterians embraced the American Revolution with such fervor and took an active and vital part in it.

The very typicality of Moses Waddel fitted him to be a leader among the Scotch-Irish. Contemporary sociological studies inform us that leaders are chosen because they represent tribal values and show in their personalities the ideal of the group. Naturally they are necessarily somewhat limited in their originality, because if their views leave the tribe too far behind, they will cease to be leaders. They may lead, but only a short distance from the norm. In fact, leaders who are capable of original views need to keep that fact to themselves. If it becomes known that the leader has different views, he may be regarded as strange, certainly not as a leader who incarnates the ideal tribal values. The best leader is he who can fulfill the cultural ideal while directing his creativity towards further verbalizing and leading in the direction that the group wishes to go anyway.

In the case of a schoolmaster like Dr. Waddel, originality of thought would especially have militated against him. Most parents, Scotch-Irish or not, prefer a conservative school teacher because they wish their children to be successes in terms of existing values which are assumed to be right. Parents are therefore generally suspicious that originality of thought may turn their children into strange intellectuals advocating socially experimental ideas. These views have not changed. Parents then as now were benevolently philistine.

BORN

William and Sarah (Morrow) Waddel from County Down, Ireland, had sailed from Belfast with their five daughters and arrived in Charleston, South Carolina, on January 25, 1767.[1] The family was to have gone to Georgia, but a severe voyage made the ship stop at Charleston, where William Waddel was to begin life in America with fifty guineas. However, William, whose horror of the evils of the city was increased by his having five growing daughters, did not want to stay in Charleston. To a Scotch-Irish Presbyterian Charleston must have been sinfully beautiful in the spring, a city of great houses, lush gardens, enticing alleys, and beautiful mulattoes; of slaves absolutely obedient to every whim; of garden paths shaded with moss and flowering magnolias, whispering of Voodoo, leading straight to the everlasting bonfire.

Even the one Presbyterian Church in Charleston, the Scots Kirk, was a Hanoverian Tory Church, whose minister, the Rev. Alexander Hewat, a Royalist who wrote a History of the Provinces of South Carolina and Georgia, would actually return to Britain in 1776 when the Revolution commenced. Although the Scots and Scotch-Irish shared Presbyterianism, the differences between them were profound, rather like the antipathy of the staunchly Catholic Irish and the staunchly Catholic Italians toward each other in New York. Obviously the Scots Kirk of Charleston did not offer William and Sarah Waddel a spiritual home abroad. In fact, the Kirk was probably more a source of irritation than anything else. The contempt of a poor, flamingly anti-Hanoverian Scotch-Irishman for this Kirk of rich English-sympathizing Scots can only be imagined. A trustee of the church in 1763, for example, was the Deputy Secretary of the Province, George Murray, whose wife, Lady Anne, was third daughter of the Earl of Cromarty, a Jacobite. Murray was one of the trustees who put Dr. Hewat in the pulpit.[2] "Woe," Waddel must have thought, "woe to them that are at ease in Zion."

Within the year William and Sarah departed "Babylon-on-the-Ashley" and headed for the morally cleaner air of the Scotch-Irish communities their people were making in the hills of the Carolina and Virginia Piedmont. The family traveled there by a mule and wagon borrowed from a friendly farmer who had come to town to sell his produce.[3] Since mules were a valuable commodity in those days, the family walked to ease the pull on the mule. What must the aristocrats of Charleston have thought as they saw "the elect" go by? Thousands of Scotch-Irish departed for the Piedmont in similar fashion. The Waddels settled on a farm on the South Yadkin River, a tributary of the Pee Dee River, where the Waddel family lived under the sparest of frontier conditions. In their log cabin the meals--mostly cornmeal and bacon--were cooked in a large fireplace, and water was carried from the river. Winter winds blew cold air through the logs so that the cabin was always drafty. Bugs came through screenless windows in the spring and summer. The only ways to travel were by foot, horse, or mule-drawn wagon.

Moses Waddel was born on this farm on July 29, 1770, in what is now Iredell County, North Carolina.[4] A sickly child, he was expected to die so that when he lived after all, he was named Moses after the patriarch who was providentially preserved through infancy to become a leader of his people. In those days a sickly boy like young Moses was likely to have to stay by the hearth near his mother and read or study to occupy himself. As a result he became a good enough scholar that at the age of seven he entered as a "half scholar" in a Mr. McKown's very plain, small school nearby. Although he stayed only six months, he shone more brightly than anyone his age, learned to read well, and to write "a fair hand."[5] A "fair hand" meant a very good one then. Legible, even calligraphic, handwriting was emphasized in those pre-machine days when many a poor boy made his living through clear penmanship as a clerk or accountant.

In 1778 the Rev. James Hall of Bethany Church, a Scotch-Irishman, established a very good preparatory academy, unofficially called Clio's Nursery,[6] from the name of the muse of history. Hall, who preached at several churches in Iredell County, was a zealous patriot. Near the start of the Revolution, he told his congregation at the end'of a sermon one Sunday that he believed it his Christian duty in the present crisis to take up arms and fight for his country. He formed a company of soldiers mostly from his parishioners and led the company so successfully that he was offered a commission as brigadier-general by Nathanael Greene but refused it.[7] He was a far cry from the Tory Dr. Hewat of Charleston and just the man to inspire confidence in the Waddels.

When William Waddel was asked to enter Moses in "Clio's Nursery," he at first refused, saying honestly that he was not able to purchase the necessary books. Books were quite expensive, and the Waddels were poor folk with seven other children to support. A Scotch-Irishman with a smart son, however, will do almost anything. Finally the combination of an intelligent boy and the opportunity to school him well made even a sober Presbyterian like William Waddel cast caution to the winds. William Waddel, "casting himself on Providence for the means," entered Moses in school,[8] where to no one's surprise he did well. In November

1779 when a new teacher, Francis Cummins, a young theology student, took over the academy, Moses received the help he needed. Clio's Nursery closed for a while when the British entered the Carolina Piedmont after the fall of Charleston in 1780. When the school reopened in 1782, however, Moses continued his formal schooling.

There is no doubt that Moses received some effective and thorough preparatory teaching at Clio's Nursery. Dr. Hall did not teach but was a thorough scholar in charge of the school. He had studied at Princeton, at that time the College of New Jersey, under John Witherspoon, the Presbyterian minister and college president who signed the Declaration of Independence. On graduation in 1774 Hall refused a mathematics professorship at Princeton to return to his home in the Carolinas to preach. But besides being a good enough scholar to be offered a professorship, he was a thrilling personality to any group of boys. Six feet tall, wide-shouldered, muscular, with a deep and resonant voice, he drilled his companies of parishioners into soldiers, and led them off to war, singing Psalms as if they were going to a Sabbath School picnic. Hall also accompanied an expedition against the Indians on the Georgia frontier during the Revolution. A scholar, a patriot, a commander of men, an Indian fighter, built like a prize fighter-- could a boy ask for more in his preacher and teacher?

It is hard not to conclude that some characteristics that all students of Moses Waddel later commented on, his air of authority, his demeanor that demanded obedience, the look that commanded--were patterned on the movements of Dr. Hall, the preacher-fighter hero of the area. Here was the model for young Waddel and others--a real man in a boy's eyes, unafraid to use violence ultimately to gain his ends, whether spanking in the school or shooting on the frontier. Hall was a frontier Christian-- strong, realistic, practical, even callous, yet devout, godly, and self-sacrificing. (He never married because a family might divert him from service to the community.) He shot the English and loved his Savior. Yet withal he was a gentleman, a graduate of Princeton, learned in the classics.

Even aside from Dr. Hall, the atmosphere for learning was good. There was, for example, the first scientific department in North Carolina.[9] Along with small classes (only five students the first year when Moses started) there was individual interest, counseling, and money from the young teacher Francis Cummings, who pushed Moses' career. There he acquired several qualities which would later characterize his own teaching: painstaking explanations carefully detailed, individual interest and attention, clever organizing, firm discipline, thorough preparation for college.

Teachers teach as they have been taught. Here in Cummins and Hall was the teaching-preaching foundation that was to make Old Moses great. The young Moses watched these men and modeled himself on them. Later on people would comment about his cleverness in organizing young men. He had learned his gift for organization from a master strategist who had organized the men of his congregation, marched them off to war, and been offered a brigadier-general's commission. Students learn not only by doing but by watching.

In the summer of 1784 when an assistant tutor in language was wanted in an academy at Camden, South Carolina, Dr. Hall recommended Moses. The boy was anxious to go, but his pious father, fearing the corruption of the city life (Camden was only a prosperous village) would not let him go. William kept the boy pure down on the farm.

Since Moses might not go sinning in Camden, a teaching position was found for him fifteen miles northeast of his father's house. For teaching seven Latin pupils and almost twenty in English, reading, writing, and arithmetic, he was paid seventy dollars a year and received free board in the houses of his four principal employers. He began there on October 15, 1784, and was regarded as "wonderfully successful" as a teacher--at age fourteen.[10] Moses' only teacher preparation was that he had been at Clio's Nursery. No doubt the boy taught his school using the methods by which he had been taught. His academic preparation was that he had completed the study of the Latin and Greek languages, arithmetic, Euclid's Elements, geography, moral philosophy and criticism, all of which he had finished by the time he was fourteen.[11]

Moses was always in delicate health. In April or May his clothes got wet in the rain, and being after all only a boy, he did not change them. To this refusal to change his wet clothes was attributed a "violent cold" that made him give up teaching and remain home until August. Then he took charge of an English school in the neighborhood where "his venerable pastor" Mr. Hall sent his niece and nephew to school to him.[12] This, however, was only a primary school. When the Waddel family had first arrived in Charleston long before, they had been bound for Georgia, and they continued to dwell on the idea of going to Georgia, undeterred by the fact it was Indian frontier country. It was Moses, however, who went there first in the latter part of 1786.[13]

BORN AGAIN

The Hebrew mind was highly personalized. The ancient Hebrew believed that the sun rose and set because God told it to do so. The universe did not follow any series of laws or change: when a man died, God took him; when he lived, God spared him. The universe was a puppet show with God pulling the strings mysteriously behind the scenes. Because there were some actions too evil for God to have done, however, a devil was necessary. The universe was then at times of stress a tug of war between God and Satan. Which tug would be stronger? Religion was like a melodrama. Waddel, like many Southerners, had a very highly personalized mythological type of Hebrew mind. Indeed the South was a "Hebraizing backwater," where people tended to interpret any situation in moralistic terms. No matter what happened, rain or drought, a religious lesson was often drawn.

In January 1787 young Moses Waddel was teaching school in Greene County, Georgia, a frontier area plagued by Indian troubles. In the summer of 1787 when the Creek Indians went on the warpath, Moses closed his school and returned to North Carolina to await peace.[1] The most noteworthy student Moses taught in Greene County was the future Rev. Isaac Grier, D.D., the first Presbyterian minister born in Georgia (Greene County in 1776).[2]

William and Sara Waddel, who were planning to go to Georgia themselves in the fall, asked Moses to wait until autumn to go back with them to Georgia. Moses, an independent-minded teenage boy, refused and went ahead without them. Moses' conscience worried him on the trip, however, because he had not waited for his parents. Then in Georgia he found that resuming his old teaching job was hopeless. The Indians had burned Greensboro, and the people in his school area had left their houses and fled to the log forts. After Moses rode a horse to Augusta to try to get a teaching job and then spent four weeks waiting for a job, he was refused. But at least the Indian raids were over, so he despondently returned to Greene County.

Here his Hebraic turn of mind became evident. Thinking over what had happened, he drew a moral lesson: his bad times had been caused by divine providence because of his disobedience to his parents. After he disobeyed, "neither much peace of mind nor any personal prosperity had attended him."[3] As a result of "God's warning" he resolved never to disobey his parents again. He never did.

This was Calvinism, not in theory, but in common social practice: if a man prospered, he was living right; if things went poorly, God was angry over the man's sins. The prosperous were those who lived right, and the poor were those who deserved it. God was behind the universe with reward in one hand, punishment in the other. Such a world view was deficient in analysis and abstraction, but it was rich in morality, imagery, and concrete action--and it was Waddel's mind set through life.

In 1788 he began teaching at another school in Greene County. When some normal, high-spirited young people in the vicinity began meeting once every week and dancing until the late hours, Waddel joined them--and even enjoyed it. But of course dancing was considered a great sin by Calvinists, and Moses realized that he was doing evil. Manfully he struggled against this sin and was finally able to give up what he called "the giddy dance."[4] Instead he spent his evenings at home reading classical books.

The key word in the Calvinists' view of sin may be found in Waddel's description of dancing as "giddy." Puritan psychology was desperately afraid of not being in control and regarded any situation that could not be controlled or that tended to undermine self-control as a sin. Therefore dancing, drinking, gambling, card playing, horse racing, betting--all were frightening sins. All of these had an element of giddiness that weakened self-control or left the outcome to chance.

Young Waddel's abnormal adolescent subservience to his parents and his fear of loss of control reveal some mental instability. His latent psychological problems were brought to a head by the revival of 1788 in Georgia. Throughout Georgia a series of revivals stressed how wicked and hopeless any man's state until he had a dramatic manifestation of God's mercy and was "born again." Moses attended these revivals and believed. He devoted his spare hours to religious reading and began spending more time in prayer. Nonetheless he recorded that at Holy Communion he felt "nothing but an awful and comfortless sense of...unworthiness."[5] He was leading the singing and praying in the worship services of his church, but he still wondered, "Am I a Christian? Have I been born again?"

One night he resolved never to sleep again until he was born again. Although he prayed and read the Bible and religious books as he awaited the miracle, he finally went to sleep with his candle still left burning. The next day at school he exhibited obsessive compulsive signs which even he would normally have not shown. He repeatedly had to leave his class during teaching to go pray but found no satisfaction from prayers. He tortured himself by such means as not letting himself drink when thirsty; if he passed a clear spring, he would not sip from it. He was too mean a sinner to deserve anything good. Now actively schizophrenic, he wrote that his "mind was greatly disturbed and distracted by unbelieving thoughts, suggested, no doubt, by Satan."[6] His hold on reality weakened: "Thoughts and temptation haunted his mind daily for months,"[7] and he himself, "How do I know there is a God? A Devil?" His earlier question, "How do I know I am a Christian?" belonged to this same psychological source.

Then one Wednesday while he was teaching school in this unsettled frame of mind, there was a thunderstorm; lightning flashed around the school house, and everything was alight with a vivid glow in an almost apocalyptic scene. As bass toned thunder rolled, Waddel knew a terrible horror because he felt that the next bolt was going to send him to hell. To the question of why God was going to strike him came the simple answer that Moses had neglected to open school with prayer. He bargained madly with God in the storm: if God would spare him, he would open his school with prayer in the future.

He never wondered why God had nothing else to do but frighten a backwoods school teacher who wouldn't open classes with prayer. As the storm hushed and the sun reappeared, the little teacher felt even more guilty and condemned by God. He went home with an even more unsettled mind, for after all he was a great sinner whom God had warned in a personal thunderstorm. He must have liked the attention, however, because he did not open his school with prayer the next day.

As often happens in the Southern rainy season, there was a thunderstorm the next day too. When Moses realized God was coming back again with more lightning, he later wrote he "felt a terror he could never describe."[8] Certain each time the lightning crackled that the next bolt would send his soul to hell, he pleaded madly with God for his life as the thunder pealed. He had learned his lesson: there would be prayer every day to open school if he lived. Naturally the storm quickly hushed, and the sun reappeared. Moses lived, needless to say, and from then on he opened his school with prayer regularly until he died.[9]

Dancing, not opening his school with prayer, and disobeying his father on a minor issue were Moses' biggest sins, the high points of his career as a sinner. Moses was never to know what a really good sin was. He had no memories of forbidden fruits, sweeter because forbidden, or the delight of scratching a forbidden itch. This lack was unfortunate because it meant that Waddel had no memories to give him sympathy and understanding for the ordinary sinner. His lack of experience made him prissy and gave him a lady's mind, schooled, refined, but dangerously innocent so that he taught boys all his life without ever having been one. But this had its good side. Waddel knew nothing, so he could rush in with a religious solution where angels feared to tread.

Not surprisingly, soon after his breakdown in the schoolhouse he physically broke down and was taken, feverish, to his parents' house where they could watch over him. He was apparently in the midst of a nervous as well as physical breakdown so that he could not work and his thoughts were gloomy--in his own words, "sometimes truly awful."[10] The obsessive compulsive symptoms became stronger to the point that he had to go to a grove of trees to pray on his knees twenty or thirty times a day. After each prayer he felt the same as "when I left" and would do it all over again.[11]

In October he developed influenza, his second sickness, but recovered to the point that on November 15 he was able to attend Holy Communion at Bethany Church. There he felt at last before the Lord's Table "a sweet serenity of soul I think I had not known before."[12] When Moses decided soon afterwards, to become a minister, he went to see the Rev. John Springer, a widely-respected older minister who taught at Cambridge Acadamy at "Ninety Six" in Abbeville District, South Carolina. A graduate of Princeton College who had also taught at Hampden-Sydney College, Springer was the first Presbyterian minister ordained in Georgia.[13] He advised Moses to go to Hampden-Sydney College for his ministerial training.

Moses was not the first minister in the Waddel family. Although poor, his family was highly respectable-- and proud that the Rev. James Waddel of Virginia, once of Newry, Ireland, was a kinsman. In 1803 William Wirt in Letter VII of his *Letters of the British Spy* told of stumbling upon a Virginia church in a rural area and pausing to hear the sermon. James Waddel, who was preaching, was a scholar who had gone blind in 1787 and afterwards preached with increased effectiveness. Blind James consecrated the Holy Communion and preached eloquently and passionately on the sufferings of Jesus Christ in the crucifixion. Wirt compared the preaching to what he understood of the sublimity of Massillon and the force of Bourdaloue, preachers to the courts of Louis XIV and XV.[14] What was more, the Rev. James Waddel in his own way proved to be an original and unconventional thinker who fitted his deed to the thought. Although a devout Calvinist, he shocked, even horrified, the pious puritans in Virginia by permitting his daughters to learn and dance the minuet.

HAMPDEN-SYDNEY

Hampden-Sydney College was not technically Presbyterian and was definitely not supposed to be narrowly denominational. It was founded in 1776 as a school to turn out Christian men who would serve the community. This goal was a new and liberal conception in the South, where most colleges were founded solely to further denominational schemes. Hampden-Sydney's first president, Samuel Stanhope Smith, a Presbyterian clergyman, said that it was to "form good men and good citizens on the common and universal principles of morality, distinguished from the narrow tenets which formed the complexion of any sect."[1] Furthermore, although the school was founded by the Presbytery of Hanover, most of its trustees, including Patrick Henry and James Madison, were Anglican.[2] Admittedly, although Henry was an Anglican like his father, his mother had been a devout Presbyterian,[3] and perhaps because of her, Henry was sympathetic to "dissenter" causes.

President Stanhope Smith resigned in 1787 and was replaced by his brother, the Reverend John Blair Smith. The Smith brothers, the best that Virginia Presbyterianism had to offer, were indeed Scotch-Irish; but far from being ranting, raw backwoods moralists, they were gentlemen who had won the respect of the Anglican planters and lawyers who made up the establishment. John Blair Smith, a Princeton classmate of "Light Horse Harry" Lee who went to Virginia in 1775, was evangelical and devout but did not follow those amusing excesses in moral conduct that made backwoods Calvinism ridiculous. Instead of being dour and judgmental, he was animating, clever and urbane. Such men made their mark. "During the fifteen years he lived in Virginia, Presbyterianism first emerged from the group of sects tolerated by the gentry as perhaps suitable for people of no particular importance, and became popular with the ruling class," wrote the historian, Cary Johnson.[4]

The year 1787 was an important year at Hampden-Sydney for a reason absolutely no one could have guessed at the time. There began the second Great Awakening, a series of revivalistic tremors to shake American religion and change American religion forever. In the autumn of 1787 a Presbyterian student, Cary Allen, went to a revival meeting in an Anglican Church held by a Reverend Hull, who seems to have been a Methodist.[5] During the meeting he began the holy jerks, groaning, shaking, and trembling, which climaxed by his falling to the floor. Allen said he surrendered to God there on the floor, and arose changed. Shortly after, but not at this meeting, three others were converted, and soon the four were holding secret prayer meetings. This kind of emotional prayer meeting naturally could not remain secret long.

23

A Faithful Narrative by Jonathan Edwards, a work describing the conversion of many hundreds in Northampton, Massachusetts, in 1735, describes something near this: "Commonly persons' minds immediately before this discovery of God's justice are exceedingly restless, and in a kind of struggle and tumult, and sometimes in mere anguish; but generally as soon as they have this conviction...they then come to a conclusion within themselves that they will lie at God's feet, and wait his time, and they rest in that, not being sensible."[6] That there were some defects in this system of grace was freely admitted in Chapter 5, "Defects and decline of the work," in which Edwards said, "a gentleman of more than common understanding...exceedingly concerned about state of his soul...kept awake night, meditating...so that he had scarce any sleep at all" finally decided his condition as a sinner was hopeless and cut his throat.[7]

This excessive emotionalism naturally disturbed urbane President Smith; however, he was wise enough not to make martyrs of the young men by turning them out. Indeed he asked them to hold their prayer meeting in his parlor, and naturally everyone wanted to come. Revivalism became the fashion, but Smith tried to keep a Presbyterian discipline of order upon it. For instance, Methodist and Baptist revivals in the area enjoyed leaping, falling down, screaming, groaning, kicking and shouting, but if any of this happened during Smith's worship services, he paused to say, "God is not the author of confusion, but of peace...you must compose yourself."[8] By such means Smith was able to contain revivalism at Hampden-Sydney. In fact, by dignity and order, he used it to some advantage. But it could not be contained elsewhere. The revival spread to another Presbyterian school, Liberty Hall (later Washington and Lee), and then to Kentucky, where the Presbyterians began revivals but soon found them too much to cope with.

The Presbyterian ministry could not contain the emotional common folk, but the Methodists and Baptists used this to their advantage.[9] From Kentucky waves of camp meeting revivalism spread phenomenally at the same time that another phenomenal rise and spread occurred, that of corn-based whiskey or Bourbon, which was first made in the late 1780's in Georgetown, Kentucky, by a Baptist minister, the Rev. Elijah Craig. At camp meetings one might enjoy the spirits of one's choice.

Although John Blair Smith left Virginia in 1790 to accept a call to the Pine Street Presbyterian Church of Philadelphia, his spirit was to be the prevailing one at Hampden-Sydney in the time Waddel studied there. The emotions of revivalism were encouraged but under control. To be a Presbyterian clergyman was to be a gentleman whose main duty was service to the community.

Waddel entered Hampden-Sydney on January 3, 1791, having spent the preceding six months on campus preparing successfully to enter the senior class.[10] Moses became friends with the new President, the Rev. Drury Lacy, who when young was pro-revivalism. In a letter to Waddel, his former pupil, dated February 20, 1793, Lacy said, "When you have an opportunity of writing tell me everything--how you were received among the old tough heads--whether you have had courage to stand to your resolution to sing Watts' hymns?"[11] But Lacy was not an innovator in all respects; he closed his letter by remarking, "Dissipation is gaining ground upon us. There has been dancing at Prince Edward Court house...may the Lord overturn, overturn, overturn...such damnable practicing."

The hymn-singing mentioned by Lacy was one of the great controversies of the day. Isaac Watts, an English Puritan, objecting to the exclusive use of Psalm-singing in Calvinist worship, introduced new evangelical themes of a cheap and sentimental nature alongside the Psalms as well as bowdlerizing the violence out of some of the Psalms. These hymns appealed to the revivalist party. But when Watts's Psalms were sung in 1778 in Poplar Tent Church in Waddel's North Carolina, one of the conservative elders (probably a "tough head") walked out, bellowing, "Give us none of your new lilt."[12]

Instead of the paper requirement of two years' residency, Waddel completed his studies in eight months and twenty-six days to finish in September 1791. William Henry Harrison, also listed as one of the eight seniors in the class of 1791, stayed at Hampden-Sydney a shorter time than usual because his parents withdrew him in fear of the possible religious excesses of revivalism.[13] George M. Bibb, a future Secretary of the Treasury, was also a member of this senior class.

Waddel was licensed to preach by the Presbytery of Hanover. As was the custom, this licensing was done by the gentlemen of the Presbytery after long and grueling examinations to check competency in Latin and Greek, Calvin's theology, the Presbyterian form of church government, knowledge of the Bible, and the Westminister Confession of 1647 and its catechisms. These licensing examinations, which usually lasted hours, were too thorough, rigidly creedal, and deadeningly catechetical. The Presbyterian clergy, hair-splitting medieval scholastics often, were prepared to argue a text for hours. Getting licensed was an emotional experience as well as an intellectual accomplishment. Forty-one years later Waddel could still remember in his diary the exact day-- May 12, 1792--he was licensed by the Presbytery of Hanover.

When the Rev. James Waddel proudly invited his young kinsman to preach his first sermon at his church, Moses accepted. As an old man he recorded in his diary, "Forty-four years ago this day (May 16, 1792) I preached my first sermon in Orange County, Virginia, in the church and presence of James Waddel. The text was John 12:26. If any man serve me, let him follow me; and where I am, there shall also my servant be."[14]

THE LOW COUNTRY

After graduating from Hampden-Sydney Moses Waddel went to the South Carolina Low Country and lived with the family of Mr. Thomas Legare, a pious aristocrat of Charleston.[1] Charleston being the center of culture in the deep South, it was natural that a bright young man should seek out the center of learning and refinement to polish himself and see what the world was like.

The young Moses setting out to exemplify his calling was a pleasant-looking young man. His height--five feet, nine inches--was above average for the smaller people of the time. He was "nearly perfect" in limb and muscular and stocky in build. His brain was larger than most, and he had grey eyes, dark hair, and bushy eyebrows which he drew so close together when he was angry that they overlapped. Underneath them was an eagle nose.[2] He had a tapering and elegant face.

Moses preached at several churches around Charleston, supplying the pulpits one Sunday each in the churches at Dorchester, James Island, Johns Island, and Wadmalaw.[3] It was not unusual for smaller congregations to have part-time ministers to come in to serve one or two Sundays each month. Sunday meant two long sermons, one in the morning and one in the afternoon, with the members of the congregation bringing food with them and eating dinner on the grounds between services. Between services, in fact, was a great social occasion when much plantation-visiting went on.

Waddel probably preached at the White Meeting House of Dorchester, a now-vanished town on the Ashley River eighteen miles from Charleston,[4] founded in 1696 by Puritans from Dorchester, Massachusetts.

Members of the White Meeting House were originally Congregational but were served by Presbyterian ministers in the South. Most of the Puritans of Dorchester moved in 1752 to Georgia, where they organized Midway Church in Liberty County in 1754. This church, called the "cradle of the Revolutionary spirit in Georgia," produced two signers of the Declaration of Independence, Lyman Hall and Button Gwinnett.[5] The remnant of the Dorchester congregation, however, remained in South Carolina, where they were served by Waddel. Since New England Congregationalists and the Presbyterians were Calvinists alike, they often interchanged ministers. It was not unusual for a Presbyterian minister to serve a Congregational church.

The church at Johns Island was founded between 1706 and 1710, and a wooden structure, still standing, was built by Calvinists in 1719, where the family of Thomas Legare attended services when they were not in Charleston. The church was a plain white pioneer effort, unmistakably Georgian. Johns Island being a part of the rich rice and indigo culture of coastal South Carolina, the Presbyterian Church there included well-to-do planters such as Thomas Legare and wealthy merchants. Being near Charleston, the island was socially a province of it. Legare was a member of the Circular Congregational Church during the part of the year that he lived in Charleston. This was the very same well-to-do society that Moses' father had rejected with his feet twenty-five years ago. It was ironic that the son of William who walked besides the mules should be back in twenty-three years as a valued and respected spiritual leader living with a lordly and aristocratic Legare. Waddel's residence at the Legares symbolized the social jump he had taken because the Legares were among the best-cultivated families in Charleston. They were aristocratic, often wealthy, and in the Southern fashion kin to practically everybody who was anybody. Furthermore, Thomas Legare was a very pious gentleman, who had fallen under conviction of sin at age seven, not unusual in those times. Legare remained convinced of his sins but deeply despondent about grace until converted by his friend, George Whitefield, a famous English preacher.

The popular religion of the time was not a positive one but was founded primarily on the fear of hell. People became church members to escape hell, as a form of fire insurance. Whitefield, approved by such prominent American Calvinists as Jonathan Edwards and the Tennents, was a prime example of a hellfire orientation. Sometimes when Whitefield got in the pulpit to preach, he looked around for a minute or two, then burst out crying. Later on in his sermon he explained that he was crying for all the unconverted people before him who were going to hell. A friend of his remarked that he wept in nearly every sermon.[6] In New England when George Whitefield preached before Edwards in 1740, Jonathan Edwards wept during the entire sermon. The choice sight of both of them boiling over would not have been noticed, however, since when Whitefield preached, "shrieking, crying, weeping, and wailing were to be heard in every corner; men's hearts failing them for fear, and many falling into the arms of their friends." As Whitefield saw all this on November 2, 1740, he remarked, "A sense of God's goodness overwhelmed me."[7]

Although not all Calvinist ministers were like this, it was Whitefield, the great revivalist, who must have been Waddel's example because he was a hero of Thomas Legare, whose evangelical and theological frame of mind was definitely shared by Waddel. Waddel's preaching was considered blunt, plain, unadorned, and simple, like Whitefield's. Also just as Waddel preached as a form of therapy for his mental depressions, Whitefield used "perpetual preaching" as remedy for physical sickness, and in one case inflammatory sore throat. Whitefield indeed said, "When this grand catholicon preaching fails, it is all over with me."[8] Whitefield and Waddel were even equally awed by thunder and lightning. Whitefield said that the thunder was "the voice of the Almighty as he passed by in anger" and that lightning was "a glance from the angry eye of Jehovah." In a scene reminiscent of Waddel's reaction, when a thunderstorm became very bad during one of his sermons, Whitefield came out from behind the pulpit, got on his knees to recite, "Hark, the Eternal rends the sky!" and then had everyone sing the Doxology.

Religiously Waddel was a positive supporter of Calvinism, but when he examined his faith, he found it lacking in one respect: its denominational narrowness. He preached in Methodist and Baptist churches freely. This he probably picked up from Whitefield, who said that in heaven they did not know the names of denominations but that all were Christians.[9] The narrowness of some Presbyterians may be seen in that tokens were necessary for Presbyterians to receive Holy Communion. The elders of the congregation met with the pastor as moderator, decided who was righteous enough to receive Communion, and then gave these people tokens. When Holy Communion was served on tables in the aisles of the meeting house, only righteous Presbyterians with a token of admission were allowed to sit there.[10]

Waddel's view of Holy Communion, which he referred to as the "Eucharist," was very high. When he consecrated the elements, a loaf of unleavened bread and a chalice of wine, he genuinely believed that his consecration made Christ present spiritually but not physically at the Lord's Table. (Alongside his high opinion of the spiritual presence went a paradoxically low opinion of its physical presence. He began using grape juice in the sacramental wine chalice of his parish at Willington, South Carolina, on May 16, 1835.)

The order of service that Waddel used was simple: a short prayer, the reading of a chapter of the Bible, a long prayer, a hymn, the sermon, a prayer, the collection, a Psalm, and the Benediction.[11] The sermon was at least an hour in length. The long prayer might run up to fifteen or twenty minutes.

Waddel was a poor, provincial boy from the back-country who served well-to-do churches. The nearest indication of their wealth is that an 1838 inventory showed the Johns Island Church owning one plantation, twenty black slaves, a summer manse, $12,000 in bonds, $2,000 in stocks, two summer church buildings, and a

winter church building in the middle of the island.
To a boy born in a log cabin such ecclesiastical wealth
must have seemed like Babylon revived. Worse by far,
in his eyes, was that everywhere he looked he saw excess,
extravagance and ease--a society that gloried in material-
ism, hedonism and self-indulgence, though it was also
cultivated and charming. Indeed Charleston and its surrounding coastal areas, a gumbo-like English combination
of culture, snobbery, and slavery, resembled Barbados
or Jamaica far more than the rest of the young United
States. Waddel had never seen anything like it. The
dramatic difference between the coastal tidewater area
and the Piedmont, between upcountry and Low Country,
came as a shock to him. Even Virginia had not prepared
him to face South Carolina in its most feudal and indolent
splendor.

    In Low Country South Carolina the most important
economic unit was the plantation, a bastard derivation
of the English manor system. Upon these manors was
erected an aristocratic and class-conscious way of life
whose feudal atmosphere permeated every aspect of society.
Anything that needed to be done in the community awaited
the will of the great plutocratic planters. Manual
labor was often held in contempt as something for Negroes.

    In upcountry South Carolina and North Carolina, by
sharp contrast, the important economic unit was the
small farm. To get anything done in the community,
these small farmers had to covenant or contract with
each other to plan it and then work together to accomplish it. The social atmosphere, though rougher, was
more democratic, republican, and independent. Life was
plainer, harder, and maybe because of lack of money,
more moral. That every man should labor was looked
upon as such a necessity that anyone who did not work
was considered dishonorable.

    Low Country South Carolina was absolutely too
much for young Moses; the pioneer in him revolted, and
he rejected Charleston as completely as John C. Calhoun,
his pupil, was to reject it later. Charleston was high
culture of a type, but to Waddel learning was not an
end in itself but an aid to moral excellence, a hand-
maiden to virtue. From such a medieval theological
viewpoint, of course, Charleston had failed, and Waddel
would be no part of it. It offended both the republicanism of his frontier upbringing and the morality of his
Calvinistic upbringing.

    Waddel could have remained in his rich coastal
parish, become a comfortable society preacher, and
married quite easily into one of the rich and pious
Presbyterian families of the coast, founding a dynasty
of his own. (The <u>South Carolina Gazette</u> of August 26,

1745 included the following: "Rev. Mr. Grant, pastor of the Scots Kirk in this town was married to Miss Elizabeth Martin, a handsome young lady, with a pretty fortune.") But Waddel, made of sterner stuff, made perhaps the great moral decision of his life, to leave the coast and return to the upcountry hills. He made up his mind to turn his back on the wealth of Charleston, refuse to settle for a life of quiet selfishness, and return to the frontier.

As his father years before Moses departed the "sinful city." Moses' views were more sophisticated and elaborate than his father's, but the outcome was the same. It is safe to say that the eighteenth-century Moses felt that if Charleston and the coast were the best in civilization that America had to offer, then America had to start over. He received a call from a small upcountry church and left. Although Waddel was actually only twenty-four years old at the time he shook the dust of Charleston from his feet, he had become as old--and as bitter--in moral outlook as any bearded Jeremiah.

Waddel adamantly refused to return even when the congregations of Johns Island and Dorchester tried to get him back. A letter from Thomas Legare dated September 29, 1796, states that John's Island has endeavored to call him as pastor again.[12] Even as late as March 6, 1798, two years later, Legare was still trying to persuade him to return to the congregation of John's Island.[13] Legare notes in a postscript to the same letter that his old congregation at Dorchester was trying to call Waddel again also. It is evident that as a pastor Waddel left behind a successful work in terms of piety, because Legare also pointed out that Waddel raised the level of James Island to that of a religious people, and therefore ought not to give up on the Low Country. But in the eyes of Waddel the Low Country was a profane land. He lifted his eyes--literally--to the hills.

When Waddel, as an earnest and surely pure young bachelor, left behind the fleshpots of Charleston, escaping a good deal of temptation, he had no idea of his future meeting with a pretty, dark-eyed maiden who was to send the prophet to prayer. Marriage awaited him in the hills.

CARMEL

Moses accepted a ministerial call for one half his Sundays from Carmel Church in Columbia County, Georgia. At the ceremony ordaining him as pastor of Carmel on June 6, 1794, the sermon was preached by Moses' good friend and former teacher at Clio's Nursery, the Rev. Francis Cummins. Cummins' sermon, entitled "The Spiritual Watchman's Character, Call and Duty Described: Together with the Duty of the People under his Care," was considered quite a triumph and later printed, all nineteen pages, at the request of the Presbytery. There was some common sense in it: "discourage not your pastor...by censorious remarks on the pitiable but common frailties of his human nature," and it also cautioned the congregation to be sure to pay the minister a fair salary promptly. Cummins pointed out the plight of a minister with a meagre salary and a numerous family "whose wants are daily appealing to his...heart."[1]

The economic suggestions to the congregation were wasted. Waddel decided, like the Apostle Paul, to accept no money for his ministry. As St. Paul had made his living as a tentmaker, Moses also intended to make his way without charging the church. It is not written down exactly when but early in his ministry he began refusing to take any salary.[2] In fact, the desire to make his own way was probably one of the reasons he set up an academy. His church was a half-time ministry for which he charged nothing, except for marriage ceremonies. Since he needed a way to make a living but also wanted to serve his community in a Christian way, the logical choice was a school.

The idea of opening an academy was far from original. Almost every Presbyterian minister of the time did this not only to supplement his salary but to follow Presbyterian church teaching.[3] The idea of a school in the shadow of every church was advocated by the founder of the Church of Scotland, John Knox. Log cabin academies proliferated in Scotch-Irish settlements. Clio's Nursery, where Waddel attended, had been such an academy opened by the Rev. Mr. Hall. The famous original of these Presbyterian academies was the Rev. Gilbert Tennent's "Log College," which anticipated the College of New Jersey at Princeton, the center of Scotch-Irish intellectual life in America. The "Log College" at Neshaminy, Pennsylvania, taught many early American political and ecclesiastical leaders and was imitated on the frontier by ministers who also taught a classical academic curriculum under crude conditions.

The log cabin academy was inexpensively constructed and quickly built. Usually when the Scotch-Irish community found a minister, he would also serve as schoolmaster. Presbyterian clergy were rare because of the stiff academic training required, so obtaining a clergyman was not always easy. But once a ministerial schoolmaster was found, a subscription was taken in the community to cover school building materials. The members of the rural community next came together for a "raising," to have a party and to work. Although the "raising" was a social event that few pioneers care to miss, the simple log structure was still usually raised in one day. Sometimes the log structure served as a church as well as a schoolhouse. Since Calvinist churches were built like lecture halls anyway, their double use as schoolroom and auditorium for preaching was quite practical.

Carmel Academy, which Waddel opened in 1794, was about two and one-half miles from the present site of Appling, Georgia, near the Savannah River. Young Moses was carrying a heavy work load, preaching twenty-six Sundays of the year at Carmel Church and the other Sundays wherever he was wanted or needed up and down the river, then teaching at Carmel Academy during the week and probably farming on the side. Most of his life he did all three.

The most famous student of Carmel Academy was William Harris Crawford, U.S. Senator, Minister to France, Secretary of War, and candidate for the Presidency. Except for a period long afterward when Crawford read law, Carmel Academy provided his only formal schooling and probably caused a good deal of the change in Crawford from country bumpkin to gentleman by "modifying the outlook of the youth, which doubtless would otherwise have been that of the plantation's squires roughened by contact with a crude frontier."[4] In all his lifetime of work with students Waddel frequently declared that he thought most highly of the intellectual ability of W. H. Crawford, possibly because when Crawford went to Waddel, he was around twenty-one or twenty-two, just two years younger than his teacher. Crawford was soon made chief usher or monitor of the school, assisting Waddel. Crawford even acted the lead in the school play of Carmel Academy, always presented at commencement as a part of the festivities to entertain the visitors.

As a Puritan, of course, Waddel was strongly against theatre. But by some strange dispensation of the religious mentality certain plays--classical, Shakespearian, modern with classical themes--were not considered theatre. Shakespeare was approved even though Romeo and Juliet throbbed with romantic passion, and the violence in Hamlet literally left the stage strewn with corpses. Aristophenes' gutter talk was accepted in Greek as classical but shocking in contemporary Anglo-Saxon English.

The school play for the Carmel Academy was Joseph Addison's Cato, first performed in London in April 1713. Dr. Samuel Johnson, the English critic, said that this play, first performed in 1713 contains "just sentiments in elegant language" but added that the characters are weak, that there is no character development or suspense, and that Cato himself is a "being above our solicitude."[5] However, Cato does observe all the classical principles, the unities of action, time and place, the proper moral sentiments, complete propriety of manners, and strict decorum among the characters. It therefore seemed a good play for young people, especially since Cato was the kind of man whom Seneca described as "a brave man matched with evil fortune" who remained "erect amidst the ruins of the republic."[6]

Although Crawford consented to play Cato, he was very tall, ungainly and awkward--not the picture of noble patrician elegance the role demanded but an adolescent ploughboy falling all over himself: "It was a matter of great sport, even during rehearsals as his young companions beheld the huge, unsightly usher, with giant strides and stentorian voice, go through with the representation of the stern, precise old Roman."[8]

The audience was to find the play a comedy in the end--predictably, as the lines are far from true to life. During most of the play, however, the awkward and ungainly Crawford managed to negotiate such scenes as Cato's address to the Roman senate and even the scene in which Cato, the stoic, soliloquizes on the unimportance of death.[9] But Crawford, of course, had no experience of death and could not fake such a conception. Therefore when the time came for Cato to throw himself on his sword and die nobly as the last of the Romans, the dying groan, which came from off stage where fear of the audience could not act as a damper, was an unbelievably loud, hearty and long bellow or even a howl. The practical pioneer folk who had been watching a neighbor's boy spouting high-flown phrases on an outdoor stage in a forest clearing, suddenly heard young Billy howling like a hog-caller, and they finally enjoyed a well-deserved collapse into unrestrained fits of laughter.

Although Waddel always tried to keep a straight face in such circumstances, believing that the younger boys needed to take the monitors seriously, it was probably difficult to do on this occasion and on many others. Augustus Longstreet in later years told about a new monitor whom he did not like because he thought the new monitor took himself too seriously. Young Longstreet, translating a Greek grammar, carefully tiptoed behind the earnest monitor all day long, conjugating Greek as he commented, "Tupto, tupteis, tuptei (of all the monitors) tupeton, tupetou (that I ever say in my life) tuptomen, tuptete (this monitor takes the lead) tuptosi (rather rowsy)."[10] When the irritated monitor reported Longstreet to Waddel, Old Moses tried to listen gravely with a straight face and maintain the dignity of the monitors before the younger boys. During the difficult struggle, Waddel's face went through all sorts of expressions to keep from bursting out laughing, but "Gus" was finally dismissed without punishment. Waddel found in teaching he had to appear graver even than he actually was.

Although Carmel Academy lasted only two years (1794-96), three future United States senators studied there--W. H. Crawford, Thomas W. Cobb, and John C. Calhoun--as well as others who were not in the public eye. Calhoun studied for a time at Carmel and then returned to another of Waddel's school for a longer time later. Indeed, perhaps starring in Cato helped W. H. Crawford get elected since as the Georgia historian E. Merton Coulter wrote, "It was necessary to amuse Georgians, not convince them, if their votes were to be secured."[11]

Crawford, Secretary of the Treasury under James Munroe, once told President Monroe he was a "damned, infernal old scoundrel," and Monroe, whose patience was also at an end, hit him with a poker.[12] Evidently the star of Cato had not found a compatible philosophy in the detached and dignified stoicism of that "last of the Romans."

MARRIAGE

Catherine, a sister to the future statesman, John C. Calhoun, was no lightheaded and coy Southern belle of the magnolias. Few, if any, upcountry women were like that. Indeed the Piedmont people looked with contempt on (as they saw them) the syrup-mouthed Charleston girls who pretended they were feeble-minded. The women of the hills stood taller, were inclined to say what they thought, looked a person straight in the eye, had a deportment that was quieter and more dignified, a manner that smacked more of the woods and stars than of finishing schools. Catherine especially was ethereal to Moses.

Catherine probably was not beautiful, to be sure; the Calhouns tended rather to be handsome, intense, haunting, tall with black hair and deep eyes and shy smiles. But in any case Catherine haunted the young preacher who came to stay the night with the Patrick Calhoun family. In deep reverie Waddel stood with his back to the Calhoun fireside and looked at their "interesting" daughter.[1] He was vaguely aware that her brother, twelve-year-old John, was opening the door, peeking in shyly to see the preacher, then, curiosity taken care of, running before the preacher saw him and asked him catechism questions. Young John probably needn't have hurried; Waddel's eyes were riveted on the lovely Kitty.

When a minister came to visit, it was the custom in those days for him to catechize all the members of the house from the father to the six-year-olds. Fisher's 530-page <u>Shorter Catechism</u> of 1765, the one generally used, had 107 main questions and answers-- and after the first question alone there are forty-nine minor questions elucidating the first major question. On a typical minister's call to pious Presbyterians, the agenda would be a quick family romp through the 107 main questions, followed by <u>Bible</u> reading, the minister's lengthy exhortation or short sermon to the family, and at least twenty minutes of prayer. There is no reason to believe this normal procedure was not used when the Rev. Mr. Waddel stopped at the Calhouns. There is reason to believe Moses watched the "interesting" young Miss Calhoun through the whole thing.

That night Moses Waddel had a dream that he married Catherine Calhoun and that she died within a year.[2] Such dreams and stories of being granted "the second sight" were common among the Scots and Scotch-Irish. John Knox himself believed he had the second sight and saw it as one of God's proofs of his ministry to Scotland.

Catherine Calhoun was not Moses' first romance. At Hampden-Sydney he had asked his cousin, Elizabeth Pleasants, to marry him, but her parents, not wanting to risk their daughter on the wild frontier of Georgia, had forbidden it.[3] Although disappointed, young Waddel got over it and in a few years had forgotten his college romance.

Patrick Calhoun, father of Catherine and John, was a very successful pioneer, one of the leaders of the Ninety-Six District in upper South Carolina. The owner of a frame house (impressive because rare in an area of log houses), five farms, and thirty-one slaves (only one slave owner had more), he was also first cousin by marriage to General Andrew Pickens, a hero of the American Revolution, and the most prominent man in the area.[4] Patrick and his wife, Martha, had five children. Catherine was the only daughter. The four boys were William, James, John, and Patrick.

Patrick Calhoun was not only a tough frontiersman, an Indian fighter whose mother had been killed by Indians in a massacre, but also a devout Presbyterian, a founder of Long Cane Church, a Bible reader, an honest man. All in all, he was a hard man who would have understood Cromwell's advice, "Pray and keep the gun powder dry."

Moses Waddel stayed at the Calhoun house because hospitality was the custom in those days when taverns and hotels were rare. The favor was mutual: isolated country hosts were glad of a new face and eager to hear news of the outside world. The Secretary of State of the Confederacy, Robert Toombs, expressed the Southern attitude of the times when he rebuked the people of his village of Washington, Georgia, for wanting to put up a hotel: "If a respectable man comes to town, he can stay at my house; if he isn't respectable, we don't want him here at all."[6]

Moses met the Calhouns when he visited Abbeville, South Carolina, to preach in Long Cane Church, in which the Calhouns were members. Preaching the gospel up and down the Savannah River, the main transportation line from Savannah to the mountains, was good publicity for Mt. Carmel, the school young Waddel had opened down the river near Augusta.

Moses, whose love for Catherine Calhoun would not wait, proposed to her, and she accepted. After the marriage date was set, a letter came to Moses from Elisabeth Pleasants, saying that her parents had been persuaded to accept the frontier and that she could now marry him.[7] But Moses now had eyes only for Catherine Calhoun, and despite the ominous dream, young

Moses and Catherine were married early in 1795. He took her to his log cabin school in Columbia County, Georgia, across the river and a few miles up from Augusta.

Catherine Calhoun, a woman of some knowledge, taught the young ones in the primary school and assisted Moses in school. She became accustomed to the log house that was by no means as fine as the one she had left, to students always underfoot, and to a new husband. The two seemed happy. Into their school the two of them welcomed a new student, her younger brother John, who lived with the Waddels and every day went to school with his teacher brother-in-law. This was a halycon time; the young Waddels, newly married and discovering each other, had a school with a future and were living in unspoiled if crude forest surroundings, now free from the fear of Indians. In the school Moses had the challenge of bright and promising young minds to teach.

But the ominous dream was true. Catherine Calhoun Waddel died in childbirth on April 10, 1796, and the baby, a daughter, died soon after. At twenty-six Moses saw his expectations of life shattered. Waddel dissolved the school and departed, half-crazed with despair, for a six-week preaching mission in the forests. He left fourteen-year-old John Calhoun unsupervised at home with only a few negroes as he set out to roam the forest and stand on rocks and stumps to preach to Indians, trappers, a few isolated cabin people, and the trees and the wind.

When Moses finally remembered to go back to check on John at the end of six weeks, he found that where as other boys would have used the free time in playing or loafing, young John, to whom books were as whiskey to an alcoholic, had headed straight for Moses' books. He had read by candle and firelight and had gotten up as soon as it was light to read more--in such books as John Locke's On Human Understanding.[8] On the verge of a nervous breakdown, John was sent back to his mother in Abbeville. Yet he would return to Waddel's school later to prepare for Yale College. John C. Calhoun had had his first long drink at the spring of knowledge.

Moses did have a nervous breakdown followed by a physical collapse very much like the one that preceded his conversion and those that he was to have all his life. He had to give up his academy, and although he continued as half-time pastor, he devoted himself mainly to restoring his nerves. In 1796 a trip on horseback to the Presbyterian General Assembly at Philadelphia, to which he was a delegate, seems to have helped restore his health. According to a newspaper announcement in 1797 Moses finally was back teaching and running the Columbia County Academy in Georgia.* His life was becoming normal again. When he heard from friends that Elisabeth Pleasants was still unmarried, he contacted her and found that indeed she was still unmarried at the rather then old-maidish age of thirty. When he proposed to her again, she accepted, this time with no family objections. When they married in 1800,[9] she brought some Virginia slaves with her as a dowry, the first slaves Waddel ever owned.[10]

Eliza and Moses Waddel had a workable marriage and raised six children to adulthood: four sons, James Pleasants, Isaac Watts, William Woodson and John Newton; and two daughters, Sara and Mary Anna.[11] (It was in keeping with his predilection for sentimental and popular hymns that Moses named two of his sons after hymn writers.) They probably lost at least one son, Moses, Junior, as a child.

Eliza Waddel's temperament, quite unlike that of Moses, was mild and gentle, and she enjoyed the company of her children as companions. Moses on the other hand, did not encourage familiarity[12] and was indeed rather a cold and distant disciplinarian of a father His children, when young, never felt he cared for them because he was never demonstrative. Only as an adult would John Newton, his son, assume that Moses "doubtless felt a warm affection" for his children. But his son did at least feel his father loved Eliza.[13]

After their marriage Moses and Eliza settled in Columbia County for a few months, then moved in 1801 to Vienna, South Carolina, where Moses set up his academy until 1804, when he finally moved it to Willington, South Carolina, where Catherine Calhoun had come from and where her family was still quite prominent. In that region Catherine's family and friends no doubt compared Eliza to Catherine many times, as it would have been only human for them to do. Eliza was undoubtedly a patient and tactful woman, or soon learned to be one.

Although Elizabeth Waddel was supplied by house slaves brought with her from Virginia, she did not have an easy life. As Waddel's wife she had to help in the practical affairs of the school, rear her family, look after her husband, and keep "lodgers." Since there were no dormitories, neighboring families supplemented their income and showed loyalty to the local school by boarding some of the students. The headmaster's wife naturally had to do her share of the boarding. Nor can it be forgotten she had to do her share in the congregation as the minister's wife.

*Carmel Academy was probably changed to or redesignated Columbia Academy to get a state grant for County school.

The Waddels worked as a team, but their relationship does not seem to have been psychologically intimate. Perhaps he was incapable of it. Waddel rarely mentions his wife in his diary. One of the few times he seemed to have anything to share with her was when he went to a circus and saw the kangaroos. He was enthusiastic over them and returned home to get his wife to come look too. There is simply no record of any great sharing or romantic passion.

This lack is not surprising. Elisabeth was a second marriage; indeed when he married her, she was already something of an old maid, and he was an emotionally burned out man. His judgement in marrying her was mature and sound, for she proved an able helpmate and a good mother to his children. It is evident she loved him, was a hard worker, and had the family interest at heart. But a certain spark was not there. One of those unconscious moments of psychological illumination is given in one entry of his diary in 1825: "Friday-- nothing important but wife sick."

Elizabeth was not like Catherine Calhoun, always interesting and young in his memory. It is quite honest to say that Catherine haunted him. On April 10, 1834, four years after burying Elizabeth, who had been his wife for thirty years, he was still remembering in his diary, "This is the 38th anniversary of my beloved first wife's death." The grief was no longer fresh, but he yet paused and remembered his unforgettable Catherine Calhoun.

WILLINGTON

The last Hugenot colony to settle in South Carolina landed in Charleston in 1764. Lt. Governor William Bull appointed Waddel's future father-in-law, Patrick Calhoun, to survey a township for the French Protestants. Patrick laid out a town, New Bordeaux, not many miles below the Calhoun settlement in the Long Cane area. The original town vanished as the Huguenots spread out to farms over the area. By the time the French-speaking pastors died in the 1770's, the Huguenots were acclimated to English and began worshipping with the Scotch-Irish in the Presbyterian Church of Hopewell in the Calhoun community. Because of the fear of Indians here, the Rev. John Harris, minister at Hopewell, had preached with a powder horn around his neck and a rifle in his hand.[1] In 1779 some Huguenots built a log church near a spring a mile from the site of New Bordeaux and called it Liberty Church. Later to become a center of their Huguenot culture, the church was served for some time by the Rev. John Springer, the friend who had advised Waddel to go to Hampden-Sydney to study for the ministry.

By the time Waddel moved to Vienna on the South Carolina side of the Savannah River, Springer had moved. The churches needed a minister, and it was only natural that they turn to Mr. Waddel, who had been a good friend of former pastor Springer. Waddel was soon called by the congregations of Hopewell and Liberty to be their pastor. Such a two-church situation meant sharing Sundays between the congregations, an accepted custom in rural areas and for small churches. Getting to his churches on horseback from Vienna was inconvenient but quite possible; many other preachers traveled farther.

A Huguenot, Pierre Gibert, very prominent in the New Bordeaux colony, saw new possibilities for his community. If Waddel could be persuaded to move nearer, both Hopewell and Liberty churches would have their minister closer for pastoral calls and meetings, and the community would gain a remarkably good school for the youth. To this end Gibert went to work on Waddel and the community to bring them together. As a result of Gibert's efforts Waddel moved his manse and school in 1804 deeper into Huguenot country, to Willington, about six miles from Vienna. A log schoolhouse was built by a group of local trustees that included Gibert.

This Willington and Calhoun community area was one of three Calvinist communities in the ante-bellum South which managed to merge civilized living with Calvinist morality. One was Hampden-Sydney College in eastern

Virginia where under pressure from Anglicanism, denominationalism was transcended in the name of Christian service. Midway Church of Georgia, called "the cradle of the Revolutionary spirit in Georgia," produced an unusual number of gifted people including two signers of the Declaration of Independence. In that plantation community a lofty morality, a Calvinist, intellectual turn of mind, and prosperity could be found together. The remaining high water mark of Calvinist civilization was Willington, a school of plain living and high thinking which produced a host of luminaries who went out to serve society. Moses Waddel in some way touched the career of all these communities which were the best that Calvinism had to offer in the South.

Though not rich, the Willington area was elevated in its morality, refined in its manners, and cultivated in its preference for education more than other and similar frontier towns. This was an area prepared to enjoy and support a good school.

An Anglican pressure in Virginia had brought Hampden-Sydney around to some sort of polish and transcedence above denominationalism as the French influence softened the Scotch-Irish Presbyterianism of the Willington area. Scotch-Irish Presbyterianism needed softening; despite many fine points its Calvinism was graceless, unpolished, and dour, with a tendency to be argumentative, provincial, and morally ranting. Craggy Scotch-Irish Presbyterians might be absolute moral monuments, but what was to be done with these social monoliths in ordinary life? They were as unappealing as the inside of the Scotch-Irish churches that looked like lecture halls. Huguenots, with a heritage and temperament quite different from that of the Scotch-Irish, bought to this grim faith some grace and charm. Pierre Moragne, of the New Bordeaux colony, was said to have coupled an interest in evangelical religion with the literary tastes of a Parisian.[2] Etienne, brother of Pastor Gibert, leader of the colony, was minister of the Chapel Royal in England.

At the time Waddel moved to Willington the economy of the area was floundering. Tobacco was languishing as the chief product, cotton had not yet taken its place, and the Huguenots had failed in growing grapes for wine. As a result the people in this Willington area had to make real sacrifices for schooling. It was to their credit they made the sacrifices and to Waddel's that he offered a schooling they felt worth sacrificing for.

Fortunately the appeal of the school was not confined to local boys, and by 1806 the sons of prominent and wealthy families all over Georgia and South Carolina were in attendance. The children of the professional classes, planters' sons, the sons of governors, senators and judges were schoolmates with the poor sons of Scotch-Irish farmers whose parents stinted that their children might have "opportunities." Other families even moved to Willington to send their sons to school there. These students from outside brought a valuable cash flow to the area's sluggish economy. Waddel wrote John C. Calhoun that in the tight money period of 1812 the Academy "supplied the District with current cash."[3]

Willington, where everything was of "cheapest, roughest, plainest kind,"[4] could be divided into the school campus itself and the three-mile area around the school. It was simply a place, a rural community of adjoining farms, and not a town in the sense of rows of permanently occupied houses. In the center of the three-mile rural community was the school. In the center of the school campus on a hill was an enormous log cabin that was built like the large keep of a stockade. The first log hall contained two common rooms. The larger, which could hold one hundred fifty, served as the chapel, the main classroom, and the courtroom--in short, the room for any meeting held in the school. There was a smaller common room that held a primary school for young children. The second school, built later, had four classrooms plus a chapel but was still of log construction and plain design. It doubled as a church auditorium on Sunday.

At the bottom of the chapel-topped hill a spring gushed from the ground and gradually enlarged into a brook that wound through a forest plain of grey-bark and green-leaf beech trees. On the other side of the hill, leading to the front entrance of the hall, was the main walk of the campus, a boulevard forty feet wide and eighty feet long. And it was literally a walk since Dr. Waddel did not encourage the boys to have horses. Dr. Waddel said often, "Show me a school boy with horse, dog and gun and I'll show you a boy who will never come to anything."

During recreation hours the main boulevard served as a sports arena[6] where boys ran, jumped, wrestled, played town ball and bull pen. On Saturday in the surrounding forest the boys hunted wild turkeys and squirrels in the day and at night hunted opossums and raccoons. On either side of the main boulevard were small log (sometimes brick) study huts or carrels that the boys either erected or bought. (The going price for one from 1806 to 1809 was five dollars.) They were built well apart from one another so that studying was not disturbed by neighbors' noise. There were other log cabins farther back from the main walk for those who preferred more isolation.

There were no prescribed rules as to where a boy might study. He might study in a log cabin, where the clay chinking was taken out from between the logs for ventilation in the spring and summer. He could study in a beech tree or by the stream, or farther back in the woodlands around the clearing.

But a student had to be on hand when it was time for his class in the log hall. Classes were signaled by a ram's horn or shofar, which was used by the ancient Hebrews as a trumpet in battle and on Yom Kippur, the Day of Atonement, and according to tradition would be blown on Judgement Day. When Moses Waddel sounded it at night for bed, in the morning for prayers, and during the day for class changes, it could be heard for miles.

The Reverend Mr. Waddel's manse, the only real house near the campus, was a neat two-story farmhouse with a picket fence around it. The manse was a quarter of a mile from the school and within comfortable riding distance of his pastorates. Waddel did not always use a horse but sometimes rode in a gig, a one-horse carriage with no top and two large wheels. There was a clean tavern not far from the manse where visiting parents stayed when they brought, picked up, or came to visit their sons. Naturally parents always stopped by the manse to see Dr. Waddel and inquire about their sons' progress in studies and conduct--and in a few cases to visit with their sons, because the Waddels had some boarders. Students did not live on campus but usually at boarding-houses kept by members of the Willington community. They walked to school each day from these boarding-houses, which varied from a few hundred yards to three miles from the campus. The accommodations were often far from luxurious. George Gilmer, later governor of Georgia, stayed with a Scottish couple named Sutherland in a two-room cabin on a small piece of land.

When Colonel Thomas Taylor of Columbia, South Carolina, sent his sons to Waddel's school in 1803, he paid Waddel eight dollars a month for one boy's board.[8] By 1809 it had gone up to ten dollars including room, laundry, and firewood. Depending upon the amount paid, the boys built their own fires or had servants do it for them. For those who gathered their own firewood a horse and wagon were available. Longstreet wrote: "For more than three years of my pupilage nearly all the fuel that was consumed upon my hearth was cut from the woods by my room-mate and myself and bourne a fatiguing distance to our door.... We often followed four hours toil in this way by five hours' study on the same evening."[9]

If boys did not wish to live in boarding-houses, they lived by themselves or shared nearby log cabins, which were often called by fanciful names. One was called Castle Carberry from Maria Roche's novel, <u>The Children of the Abbey</u>. John Walker, of a more humorous turn of mind, called his log cabin Castle Tick Hill. Boys who wished to get away from Dr. Waddel's eagle eye went to board at houses far enough away--they thought--Old Moses would not visit often. Unfortunately for them, this ploy rarely worked. The Doctor usually found out about the boys who went off to play cards, drink peach brandy, and not study. However, the use of tobacco was perfectly acceptable. It was generally not smoked since chewing--and of course spitting--was custom among many of the young men, and indeed among all men of the time, including Dr. Waddel himself.

Willington had so many things to appeal to boys that A. B. Longstreet bragged that it was the finest town in the world for boys, that the boys seemed to consider all other schools "very small affairs,"[10] compared with Willington. It made parents happy too, he added, because the school provided a morally safe atmosphere, gave good instruction, enabled the boys to grow physically as well as mentally, and taught self-reliance. The impression that Willington, which was really an adolescent social experiment in freedom and self-government to produce leadership, made on everyone--boys, adults, the general public--was remarkable. On the day fifteen-year-old James Louis Petigru, the grandson of Pastor Jean Gibert who led the Huguenots to New Bordeaux, went to the school, he wrote in his diary, "This day I am to go to Willington; with joy and fear I view the vast design."[11]

Old Moses, sounder of the shofar, was the chief of the Willington community. To begin with, his school was the benefactor of the local economy, so he had behind him the power of the purse. To this he added considerable spiritual power as shepherd of the community church. He was also the teacher and leading intellectual, holding absolute power over the many schools boys who populated the area. By gathering together all the reins of his power, he had considerably more authority over his area than did many a Scottich laird over his clan or European nobleman over his manor. It was a small area but one which Waddel could control and in which he could maintain his strict code of moral and intellectual discipline. He was master of Willington.

FREEDOM AND JUSTICE FOR ALL

The design of the school at Willington was innovative and democratic in that any offender at Willington came before a working student court, where he was given a hearing before the entire school and guaranteed a trial by a jury of peers. Here the bully, the practical joker, and the merely mischievous met justice from his schoolmates.

Students were required to live within three miles of the schoolhouse[1] and were not allowed to leave this area to go to any of the surrounding villages without first obtaining permission from Dr. Waddel. Otherwise, as long as they obeyed Willington rules, which were finally written in a Code of Laws by Waddel, students had freedom to do very much as they wished, without adults hovering over them every minute, having to know where they went and why. He believed in as much freedom and as little government as necessary for good order. To police the Willington community, he did have older boys of good character act as monitors to record any offenses that were reported to them or that they saw the students commit. Waddel made it clear to the monitors, however, that he wished to be bothered as little as possible. And in fact the only power these monitors had was to record any offenses they saw or that were reported to them. But that power was not a trifling one; if a monitor wrote it down, then it became a bill and was given to Waddel when he held court on Monday morning.

In the court, which students had to attend, Waddel was judge, but the jury was made up of five students, with a different jury for each trial. The monitor read the offense, and so did Waddel. After the monitor stated his side of the case, the accused gave his side, calling as many witnesses as relevant. After both sides had a chance to speak and the full implication of the offense had become clear, Waddel read from his laws what punishment the offender would have if the jury found him guilty. The case was then turned over to the peer jury for a verdict. If the decision of the jury was guilty, Waddel served as "executioner" to administer the punishment,[2] usually spanking with a hickory stick. The number of strokes was announced by Waddel previous to the verdict, so the jury always knew exactly what was involved.

In one case before the court a smaller boy who was hit in the nose by a bigger boy hit back and reported the bigger boy's offense to the monitor. When the bill was read before the assembly, Waddel asked the smaller boy, "Did you butt (the bigger boy) in the nose?"

"I gave him a little butt," the little boy said.

"Oh, well," said Waddel, "if you take justice into your own hands, you must not appeal to me."[3] The case was thrown out. Punishment belonged to the court and not to the individual; a student who took revenge could not then demand justice because this made a mockery of justice, whose purpose was to arrest the cycle of violence. Any other verdict would have opened the community to socially approved adolescent vendettas.

While Waddel's Code of Laws has vanished, we may infer that it was based on respect for the individual, the community, the teacher, and God. This can be gathered from the interpretation of the offenses. One verdict said, "You have no right to sport with the feelings of others for your fun,"[4] and continued, "You have no right to constrain a student to leave his company, or his place or endure a stench."[5] (The offense in question was the swinging of a dead cat so that a group scattered.) Cases were made for "being idle repeatedly" and for "throwing a chew of tobacco" in a boy's eye.[6] Fighting among these rough pioneer boys was predictably the commonest problem that Waddel had to struggle with. The boys wanted to settle everything by violence.

Even though this was a school whose purpose was academic learning, however, Waddel had wisdom enough to refuse to punish a boy for a lesson badly done in class or homework unprepared. Waddel knew that if a student was willing to make an incompetent fool of himself in class in front of his friends whose respect he valued more than the teacher's, no punishment by the teacher would help.[7] If punishment for poor schoolwork came, it would have to be through the student government in a bill of "idleness" against the offender in student court. Then through group pressure something might be done. This changed the tone from that of a teacher picking on a student to that of the group's carrying out justice. In this way preparation for class work might improve.

It was the appeal of the adolescent mind for justice that Waddel understood. Plato taught that justice is to render each man his due. Adolescents, not so philosophical, are simply determined that no one else will get away with anything they can't. Although Waddel appeared to be an implacable man, he simply understood that adolescents are uncurable idealists who expect justice from their father figures. He knew that no one must be allowed to get away with anything, that justice must be blind. Of course their desire for "justice" is really based on nothing more than envy. "If he can do it, I can do it," is the adolescent cry. . Justice must punish if order and respect are to be kept. But Waddel also understood that because justice from an adult can be bitterly interpreted as "them" persecuting "us," the peer group must be involved. With a jury of peers removing the stigma of "they," justice is then fair.

To appreciate the innovation of Willington, it is necessary to be aware how brutal and oblivious of student rights most schools were at the time. The custom was to flog boys for mistakes in class to make them work harder. Schoolmasters flogged as they pleased, of course, and in practice whether a boy was punished or not depended more on the schoolmaster's mood than on the pupil's guilt or innocence. Even older high school and college students were treated largely as serfs to be directed, prodded or cajoled in what ever direction schoolmasters picked for them to go. Of course there was underneath this an often well-meaning paternalism, but there was no justice, little freedom, and very little involvement in school government. To make matters worse, the schoolmasters who exercised this power were very often not well schooled nor even intelligent men.

George Gilmer, a Waddel pupil and later governor of Georgia, had as his first schoolmaster a deserter from the British navy. When the weather was cold, he "warmed his scholars by making them join hands, and run around, whilst he hastened their speed by the free use of the switch." His third teacher was a "wandering, drunken Irishman" who "knocked, kicked, cuffed, and whipped at a great rate."[9] The teacher sometimes knocked John, another of the Gilmer boys, to the floor ten times a day. John learned to sit lightly on his seat so the first knock would send him to the floor because the schoolmaster did not beat him after he hit the floor.[10]

The atmosphere among the boys themselves in these log schools of the pioneers was typically violent. Even when a man of good character, such as Sam Houston, the future patriot of Texas, taught school in Tennessee, he kept some lead knuckles in reserve. He also kept a stick or rod to spank with. He wrote, "At noon after luncheon...I would go into the woods and cut me a sourwood stick, trim it carefully in circular spirals... with this emblem of ornament and authority in my hand... and the sense of authority over my pupils, I experienced a higher feeling of dignity."[11]

Waddel's democratic jury procedure was probably a transference of the democratic court procedure in the Presbyterian system of government. It had instructions for the trial of offenders before the session, a group of church elders, which averaged about five members in the small congregations of the time. In this conception the congregational community had rights and the church members had rights. Presbyterian court procedure in the disciplining of offending members carefully observed the rights of both. For the Rev. Waddel to make the step from church use to secular use of a democratic method he saw work successfully was not such a big transference. It took more courage and willingness to experiment than originality of insight.

The economic historian might suggest that Waddel's democratic efforts were the inevitable outcome of an up-country society in which the basic production unit was the small independent farmer. This society made democracy necessary because, in the absence of landed plutocrats, the small farmers had to band together democratically to get anything done. A historian might argue that a society so economically structured for social democracy of government by contracting members would inevitable foster democratic efforts in schools, churches, and local governments.

Whether Waddel's efforts toward democracy and justice in his school were the outcome of economic determinism or from the example of the Presbyterian system, the profit from the jury court procedure was undeniable: a high morale, a sense of community participation, the avoidance of bitterness over discipline, and, according to A. B. Longstreet, the teaching of self-reliance. This combination of justice and freedom helped to avoid at Willington the bane of all schools, "displaced goals," which occur when any institution--school, church, asylum--forgets its main goals and allows other goals, often trivial, to take precedence. In such a situation the important thing for the student becomes going for water in class, what time the class bell rings, a ball game, instead of learning and paying attention. Students at Willington who were able to keep the real school goal of learning before them, studied more than students at other schools.[12] In fact, according to a South Carolina historian who was so impressed he sent his sons there, nine out of ten students worked as hard at their studies as their health permitted.

The fact that the boys maintained at school a good sense of priorities, putting academics first, is a testimony to Waddel's leadership. But leadership was not enough. That this leadership was possible can probably be traced to the high morale and self-reliance that came from a feeling of freedom and justice for all. Of course amount of freedom and the mode of justice were comparative, but compared with other schools, Willington was far beyond its time. The students there, all of whom had had other educational experiences elsewhere, had good reason to consider other schools as "very small efforts" beside Willington.[13]

49

TEACHER

W. J. Grayson, a Willington alumnus, believed that Waddel's success in his work was largely due to the organization and government of the Academy. However, John C. Calhoun remarked, "It was as a teacher that he was most distinguished. In that character he stands almost unrivaled.... His excellence...a felicitous combination of qualities for the government of boys and communicating to them what he knew."[1] And in fact Waddel did not rely simply on any one factor. Having originated an exciting new method of school organization, he might have contented himself with being ordinary in other respects. Instead like the "felicitous combination" he was, he laid siege to ignorance on every side.

Had he been far more authoritarian than he was, he would have been a successful teacher because he was enthusiastic over his subject and had almost a missionary zeal to share learning. He was patient and tireless in his explanations, making sure that each small part was understood before he began another. In modern teaching jargon his method would be called "sequential."

He had a thorough knowledge of the subject matter. Old Moses' students recalled that he might listen with his eyes closed to a recitation in Virgil and still be able to correct any mistakes.[2] His enthusiasm for the classics was catching, provided of course there was anyone in the audience emotionally prepared to receive. Students have to be emotionally ready for a subject, as Hugh Swinton Legaré of Charleston was. One of the great classical minds of America and an editor of the Southern Review, "the most distinguished Southern journal of its time,"[3] Legare said he caught his love of Hellenistic studies from Waddel. To be sure, everyone agreed that Waddel was not a profound scholar, but he was able to impart competently, sometimes brilliantly, often inspirationally, what he knew, exactly as an excellent secondary school teacher should.

As was the custom, Waddel's principal method of teaching was oral recitation, including translating and memorizing lines from the classics. The boys went at their own speed, slow boys doing 150 lines a lesson and bright boys far more. One boy did 1212 lines in one lesson. Oral drill was a favorite of Waddel's first of all because it required no use of paper, which was so expensive in frontier days that letter writers often wrote crisscross over paper that had already been written on. Furthermore, oral drill was effective. Today we know that it takes about three reinforcements for a person of normal intelligence to learn anything, and in those days constant recitation provided enough reinforcements day after day for even the most inattentive and dense. Indeed if recitation had not been effective, it probably would have been replaced at Willington because Waddel did not fear to innovate in method.

Waddel also taught values, although he sometimes seemed unable to tell the good from the legalistic, the moral from the respectable. But for raw frontier boys, the moral emphasis was a refining experience. The transmutation of values requires not just a sermon in class but some sort of primary relationship. Waddel cultivated informal relationships by visiting the boys at night in their various log cabins and boarding houses, where he was able to evaluate their progress in an informal setting. The letters from his students to him unanimously mention a fond appreciation of his interest, his advice, his regard, his concern for their moral betterment.

In supervising he was also tactful. If he found boys idle or mischievous, he did not explode into a tirade. Instead, at chapel he would describe (mentioning no names) what he had observed, moralize on this theme, and expound the moral ruin of such a course. The guilty boys, known only to Old Moses, squirmed silently while their temporarily innocent classmates snickered.

Waddel's strenuous character-building efforts were probably the result of his belief in original sin. Like St. Augustine, he believed that childhood innocence is solely the result of children's not being physically big enough to act out their often evil intentions. Because they partook of the evil nature of mankind they had to have attention and correction to remain on the right path. Waddel's dark view of human nature is reflected in his diary: "July 12, 1824--Mr. Stanley preached from Romans 1:32--made human nature more innocent than I think the Scriptures warrant." Given his view of human nature, moral vigilance was necessary, and character building was a must. He therefore threw himself into it, riding from boardinghouse to boardinghouse in the three-mile residential area with the devotion of a Methodist circuit rider.

Since he was tactful in his visitations, listened to his students talk, cultivated relationships with them, flattered them with his presence, and gave the impression of being sincere, the boys appreciated his attention. He filled a supportive role and gave them needed ego strength so that to many he was almost a second father. In a letter former student John Walker gives a glimpse of the informality of these visits: "I was thinking what I should have said had I been leaning against the door of the castle at Tick Hill and prattling about some nonsense or other."[5] The irrepressible Walker even teased him filially in a letter from Princeton College that "his (Professor Thompson's) abdomen beats yours." Another alumnus, Ruben Langston, began a letter to Waddel, "Dear Sir, Permit me to observe to you, that of all men, next to my father, you possess the greatest share of my affections."[6] Near the time Langston wrote from Georgia, John Posey, another "old boy," wrote from Princeton, "I forget that I am the pupil and fancy myself the son."[7]

The virtues this man encouraged in his boys were, with a few theological exceptions, relatively sound common sense. Letters make clear that he talked to them about their careers, about how to be a success, about how to get along in the world. His was the sound advice that teachers usually can give honestly: to study, to obey, to work hard, not to be idle. It would have been odd indeed if an orthodox Calvinist minister had not been busily inculcating the Calvinistic virtues, particularly church-going.

David Ramsay felt that Willington's success with his two sons was due to Waddel, who "quickly finds out the temper and disposition of each student and is the first to discover aberrations from the straight line of propriety." Whatever mischief the boy was up to, was quickly "nipped in the bud."[8] Similarly A. B. Longstreet believed that Waddel's success as a teacher included "his sleepless vigilance over morals and conduct."[9] Indeed Longstreet said that Waddel brought about those changes in his own life that made his success possible. In the old days this process was called "character-building."

Waddel knew that he was a civilizer and maker of men. When he first visited "Badwell," the Petigru farm, he heard fifteen-year-old James recount a narrative in a "clear, connected manner, and in well-chosen language." Immediately recognizing the boy's potential, he said, "If I had you with me, my boy, I would make a man of you."[10] And in fact when James Louis Petigru went to Willington, Waddel did help him to develop into a brilliant lawyer and one of the sanest minds in the South. Decades later when he, practically alone, opposed secession by South Carolina, Petigru braved the almost hysterical fervor of secessionists in the name of sanity and patriotism. Waddel had kept his word. He had made a man of him.

Something genuine between teacher and student went on at Willington. Admittedly Waddel was in some ways so strange and his religion so unattractive that even a devotee like A. B. Longstreet was turned off by his rigid Calvinism. But his goodness and sincerity touched his students so that many of them frankly loved him.

Parents too like a visit from the teacher. Since Waddel could not visit, he wrote. The following letter to a parent,[11] George Jones of "Wormsloe" plantation, United States Senator from Georgia and mayor of Savannah, shows that Waddel was a master of public relations. "Mr. Telfair" had been governor of Georgia in the early 1790s. "Master Campbell" was Dr. Jones's stepson. "Master Thomas" was Jones's son (later a congressman).

>   Columbia Academy
>   15th December 1798
>
> Dear Sir,
>
> I have the pleasure of being able to inform you that your son and master Campbell are both well at present. They have improved considerably in Latin since you left them here; being now within a week's time finishing Virgil. I most earnestly wish you would send them a Latin Dictionary, a Greek Grammar, and a Greek Lexicon. As they will finish Virgil before Christmas; I wish them to enter Cicero and the Greek Grammar immediately after the Academy commences at New Year's Day. I am partly obliged to give a few days vacation at Christmas as a large number of the students wish to go home then for to see their connections. If you can avail yourself of no other mode of conveyance, I recommend to send the books by the stage-- the freight will be a triffle and their need of them will be great. I would thank you to present my respects to Mr. Telfair and let him know that his son's superior to any youth of his years whom I have ever taught both as to genius and application. I do not hesitate to say that if he lives and is continued at study, he is capable of making a figure in the republic of letters. Master Thomas is myself the pleasure of addressing a line to Mr. Telfair in a short time. I am, dear sir, in much haste.
>
>   Your sincere friend,
>
>   Moses Waddel

Inevitably there were some failures. What succeeded with one boy did not necessarily succeed with another, and though Old Moses approached from every side, some boys were lost. James Tinsley, a classmate of A. B. Longstreet, learned "a little Latin and Greek and little else." But it was also admitted that "Tinsley was erratic and defied the conventional rules of practice of Medicine and society"[12]--and even this was an understatement. Tinsley, who finally became a physician, removed a large tumour from a woman with her husband's razor because he would not purchase surgical instruments and used whatever was handy; and he never bought any medicine, always prescribing what the family already had in the house.

There were some even Old Moses couldn't reach.*

---

*The high opinion in which Waddel's teaching was held may be seen in the following ad in the Charleston Courier, May 24, 1810--"ACADEMY in Montague-street, Charleston's Green, will commence after the spring vacation on Monday the 21st instant. An assistant of Classical Talents is employed, who was educated in the Academy of Dr. WADDLE, and who has had experience in Teaching. For terms of admission apply at the Academy, or to Mr. THEODORE GAILLARD, JUN."

CURRICULUM

After looking over the classes, new students at Willington chose the subjects and level they wished to be in, and they were allowed to advance in these subjects as rapidly as they wished--as long as they maintained a minimum standard. Although classes proceeded in order, there was no set time or length; a class ended when Waddel considered the lessons learned. A weak teacher, of course, would have ruined the students with this plan of letting them out when the lesson was learned. Under a rigorous teacher like Waddel such a system was an asset because it forced students to learn thoroughly. Painstaking attention to detail, such as going over verbs and particles for hours,[1] was characteristic of Waddel. He insisted on thoroughness in school work.[2]

Waddel's academies, rather than being simply secondary schools, prepared boys for the junior year in college. Waddel's students at their best worked, usually successfully, towards passing tests that exempted them from the first two years of college. Dr. Smith, President of Princeton (Nassau Hall), said in fact that he received no scholars from any section of the United States who stood a better examination.[3] The emphasis in Waddel's school, unlike most schools, lay on the four years from high school junior through college sophomore, a distinct period in adolescent life. In the junior and senior years of high school or preparatory school when a boy begins to exhibit increasing maturity, he is still under some supervision. This progress is often arrested in the freshman year because the student is placed entirely on his own before he is really ready. The results are many academic tragedies. However, if there is some personal or continuing supervision through the sophomore year in college, then when the boy is finally turned on his own entirely as a college junior, he has reached an age of better responsibility and more maturity.

Willington, more than a high school and less than a senior college, served a vital purpose. At a time when there were no colleges in South Carolina at the time "except in name," the best substitute was first-class work at an academy, of which the most famous was Willington.[4] Substitute college work that enabled the students to take college exams and skip the first two years was the goal of many who came to Willington. After studying at Waddel's, Calhoun and Longstreet were able to enter the junior class at Yale, and McDuffie entered the junior class at South Carolina College. "In fact nearly all who were fitted at this school entered the junior class."[5]

In curriculum Dr. Waddel tried to keep abreast of the times. He wrote to his former students who had entered Princeton to find out how he needed to improve or change his curriculum to better prepare them for senior college. Having recently taken the test for credit for the first two years, they freely sent him suggestions. One student admitted to the Princeton junior class fresh from Willington wrote, "I wish you would be particular in regard to the maps, teach the coasting, divisions, relative situations, course of rivers.... They teach Murray's Grammar here. It is indeed greatly superior to any I have ever read."[6]

Classical curriculum, which despite such innovations was still the basic part of instruction, was divided into four units.* Although the content of the units is known, the names of the books are not always known. As noted above, these units were not necessarily based on a time plan; students picked their own level and went at their own speed. Willington taught a modern language, French. Willington students were also taught how to play the flute, a classical instrument.

Unit One contained Greek Grammar, Composition, and Greek Primitives, taught quite possibly from Valpy's Grammar, Well's Greek Primitives and Nelson's Exercises.

Unit Two, consisting of Greek Grammar, Composition of Greek Sentences, Translation from Greek, Analysis, Derivation and Mythology, used Buttman's Greek Grammar, Nelson's Exercises, Pickering's Greek and English Lexicon, Jacob's Greek Reader, Collectanea Minora and Majora, and Scopula and Lempriere.

Unit Three contained Greek Grammar, Composition and Translation, Latin Grammar and Composition. The books used were Homer, Potter's Greek Antiquities, Collectanea Majora, Adam's Latin Grammar, Mair's Exercises, Cornelius Nepos, Caesar's Commentaries and Sallust.

Unit Four contained Greek and Latin Grammar, Composition and Translations, Roman Antiquities. The books used might have been Ovid's Metamorphoses Expurgata, Virgil, Cicero's Orations, Horace, Persius, Juvenal, Tacitus, Excerpta Latina and others.[7]

The preparation for a class was usually 150 lines of translation,[8] and the record for homework was 1212 lines (of Horace), set by George McDuffie. The second was a thousand in one weekend, set by George Carey.[9] The results of highly motivated and intelligent boys going at their own speed was astounding. McDuffie finished

---

*This was the four-course classical education in The General Plan of Education appointed for the South Carolina Society's Male Academy, July 1827, Charleston.

his Latin grammar in three weeks, and it is certain that under Dr. Waddel he finished it to the last detail.

An important if informal part of the curriculum was the debating society. Col. Starke, a student under Waddel, said that the debating club on Friday afternoons was regarded by Waddel as a very necessary part of his scholastic system.[10] There these boys, most of whom were preparing for law, politics, teaching or the pulpit, learned to orate before others. In a day before organized sports these debates were the centers of much campus enthusiasm. The boys learned how to think on their feet, to take notes as another spoke, to apply logic, and to structure their thoughts. Successful debating for a future lawyer or clergyman might indeed prove of more practical value later than anything else.

Longstreet in <u>Georgia Scenes</u> included (though it was not a Georgia scene) a sketch of the Willington debating society. Two of its members, Longworth (Longstreet) and McDermot (McDuffie) decided to play a joke on the members. They decided to propose for debate by the society a question "which should possess the form of a debateable question" but without a particle of honest sense behind it. They composed for debate the following proposition: "Whether at public elections, should the votes of faction predominate by internal suggestions or the bias of jurisprudence?" These two intelligent young men brought the proposition up for debate. They involved others besides themselves seriously in the debate. They made pretentious fools out of everyone except one young man who said honestly, "Gentlemen, I do not understand the subject."[11]

It is noteworthy that students at Willington were capable of such intellectual jokes. The irony of the joke's intent, the complexity of its composure, the sophisticated use of verbiage to carry it off, the vocabulary shared by the members--all these suggest a high level of intellectual attainment and sophistication among the students of backwoods Willington.

At the time of the incidents described in Longstreet's "The Debating Society," George McDuffie, later Representative, Senator, and twice governor of South Carolina, was twenty-two years old. Yet such was his rhetorical prowess already that Longstreet could say, "McDuffie seems to me to have added but little to his powers in debate, since he passed his twenty-second year."[12] By the time he graduated from South Carolina College, which he entered in his junior year direct from Willington, "his reputation as an orator had already spread throughout the State."[13] It is then reasonable to assume that the oratorical powers of McDuffie were developed under Dr. Waddel, particularly since McDuffie had no formal education before going to Dr. Waddel.

A newspaper correspondent's description of McDuffie orating shows that he was influenced by Waddel in at least one way: they were both "thumpers." An observer records that during his sermons, Waddel's "massive fist came down upon the pulpit, with a force corresponding to the strength and energy of the thought."[14] The same tendency may be discerned in his student, McDuffie. And while Dr. Waddel's "pulpit oratory would not have pronounced him a great preacher,"[15] he seems to have been able to teach that skill. The nationally famed oratory of McDuffie, of which a sample is given here, was similar to that practiced at Willington. (Indeed in the parenthetical descriptions of McDuffie's oratory we may almost make out the instructions given to him.)

"Sir, (a thump on desk upon a quire of paper heavy enough to echo over the whole hall) sir, South Carolina is oppressed, (a thump). A tyrant majority sucks her life blood from her, (a dreadful thump). Yes, sir (a pause) yes, sir, a tyrant (a thump) majority unappeased, (arms aloft) unappeasable, (horrid scream) has persecuted and persecutes us (a stamp on the floor). We appeal to them (low and quick), but we appeal in vain (loud and quick). We turn to our brethren of the north (low with a shaking of the head), and pray them to protect us (a thump), but we t-u-r-n in v-a-i-n (prolonged and a thump). They heap coals of fire on our heads (with immense rapidity)-- they give us burden on burden; they tax us more and more (very rapid, slam-bang, slam-- a hideous noise). We turn to our brethren of the south (slow with a solemn, thoughtful air). We work with them; we fight with them; we vote with them; we petition with them; (common voice and manner) but the tyrant majority has no ears, no eyes, no form (quick), deaf (long pause), sightless (pause), inexorable (slow, slow). Despairing (a thump), we resort to the rights (a pause) which God (a pause) and nature has given us (thump, thump, thump)...[16]

Yet another similarity between the two is detectable. James H. Thornwell, a Presbyterian minister noted for his oratory who was President of the University of South Carolina, 1851-1855, described McDuffie's speaking thus: "Envy, hate, scorn, revenge, all the dark and malignant passions of our nature he could summon like wild beasts...and bid them serve his purpose.... He was a man to create a revolution."[17] McDuffie was a negative and emotional orator. That McDuffie could learn from Old Moses how to be a negative and emotional orator was not at all surprising. Waddel himself was quite capable of good hellfire sermons, using such texts as

Psalm 9:17, "The wicked shall be turned into hell," and Isaiah 34:10, "It shall not be quenched...the smoke thereof shall go up forever."

The obvious defects in the curriculum at Willington did not lie in oratory or the offering of a classical education. Willington's defects were typical of the Scotch-Irish among whom "Education was zealously sought but in the scholastic tradition of the Middle Ages rather than in the liberal tradition of the Renaissance: belles lettres were absent; the Bible sufficed for literature."[18] The bad results of cultivating the head at the expense of the heart is nowhere more evident than in the education of Waddel's most famous pupil. When John C. Calhoun, in his courtship of Floride, began writing love poetry, every one of his love poems began with "whereas."[19]

Nor could Calhoun, or any other Willingtonian, generally read novels. As an adult when a woman lent him a novel, he "flipped over the pages" and remarked that it was the first novel he had ever seen.[20] Waddel's inclusion of novel-reading as one of his Calvinistic sins was really unfortunate since Calhoun, and other highly gifted students of Waddel, needed to read them desperately. Calhoun's biographer, Coit, wrote, "It was young Featherstonhaugh, who, meeting him only once, saw what those closest to him could not see. He had, declared the Englishman, 'an imperfect acquaintance with human nature... baffled by those inferior to himself.'" Coit believed that in this lay the "tragedy of Calhoun."[21] Had Calhoun read novels, he might have understood better the motivation and mind of the common herd. As it was, he came late even to the simple understanding that "few men were creatures of reason."

The education given in the Scotch-Irish Presbyterian academies was deficient not only in novels but in all modern literature and especially the fine arts. "In the realm of aesthetics," the Scotch-Irish were "practically deaf, dumb, and blind."[22] That Waddel's own aesthetic sense was deficient may be seen in his choice of bloatedly sentimental hymns to replace the Psalms in Presbyterian worship. Leyburn, social historian of the Scotch-Irish, did not feel the aesthetic deficiency to be Calvinistic since New England offered examples of a keen aesthetic sense. Rather it was Scotch-Irish. Their Presbyterian churches were concrete symbols of their lack of imagination: "One never looked to a Presbyterian church for inspiring music, stained glass, religious painting and sculpture, or poetry."[23] Naturally one could not look to Scotch-Irish academies such as Willington to teach appreciation of fine arts. True, the classics included some of the greatest examples of fine literary art, but as Clement Eaton, a leading historian of the Old South commented, "Although he, Waddel, ceaselessly taught the classics, his Calvinism made him incapable of appreciating their sensuous joy in the physical life and in the beauty of nature."[24]

No matter what subjects Dr. Waddel taught, he must have had one of the most original methods of opening the class day in history. As one alumnus, Col. Starke, recorded it: "At sunrise Dr. Waddel was wont to wind his horn, which was immediately answered by horns from various boarding houses in all directions. At an early hour the pupils made their appearance at the log cabin schoolhouse. The Doctor, entering the cabin and depositing his hat, would reappear at the door with the school horn in his hand. He then would call out loud, "What boy feels most flatulent this morning?"[25] The boy who did, had the honor of sounding the horn that served as the opening bell of the day.

LEADERS FROM THE WOODS

"The remarkable distinction of his pupils, cannot fairly be ascribed to chance,"[1] said Longstreet in his eulogy of Waddel. And in fact it was not chance but intent because the purpose of Willington was to train leaders. Waddel never made any pretense about having a school for the common man.

In one sense Willington was democratizing, however, because it gave equal educational opportunities to middle class boys in an age when a classical education in South Carolina was reserved for the sons of the upper class planters and rich merchants. Thus Willington did fit the Jeffersonian ideal of a school where bright but poor boys might be schooled and by this be given an opportunity to rise socially on their merits. George McDuffie, for example, was a desperately poverty-stricken lad who carried all his possessions tied with string in a small blue box,[2] but with schooling from Waddel, he became governor of South Carolina. Waddel aided many of these clever, indigent boys just as Francis Cummings had aided him earlier. He did unto others as he had been done unto.

A. D. Mayo suggested in a report on South Carolina education in 1896 that Waddel's Academy was founded to give the middle class boys of the Piedmont the same education as the rich planters' sons from Charleston and the low country.[3] The rich planters of the coastal area had private tutors on their plantations, and their sons often studied abroad to finish their schooling. Prosperous parents in the Piedmont, by contrast, might afford a reasonably priced boarding school and an American college, and they usually were financially strained to do that. "Keeping up with Joneses" of the low country on their large plantations was an impossibility for up-country people.

Nonetheless, if the Scotch-Irish and other citizens of the backcountry were to challenge the coastal aristocracy, their sons had to have equal schooling, that is, a classical education because this was a gentleman's education at the same time. It was still a necessity. Ramsay discussed this in his History of South Carolina, 1670-1808: "A few, with little or no classical education by...superior natural powers...have made a distinguished figure in public life. Their success, like the large prizes in a lottery, inspires false hopes in the breasts of others."[4] Willington was just such a reasonably priced reproduction en masse of a gentleman's classical education for the middle class. And "en masse" is no exaggeration; for early nineteenth century South Carolina it was a large-scale effort. From 1804-19 Dr. Waddel taught about 4,000 students at Willington.[5]

Some of these students were highly motivated, partly because they came from homes, such as Patrick Calhoun's, where Scotch-Irish ambition and backcountry resentment burned brightly. To Patrick the rise to power of his son, John, exemplified the arrival of his class and section to power and equality. Patrick had felt, accurately on both counts, that the coastal area discriminated against the backcountry, and looked down on the Scotch-Irish, and he ached for prominence and recognition. Without Willington and other academies like it, however, the poorer Scotch-Irish and the sons of the upcountry like Calhoun, E. H. Crawford, and George McDuffie would have lacked the necessary schooling to compete and rise to power. The lack of such burning ambition and resentment among the city boys from the coast may explain why "no student who entered the school between 1806-10 from the large cities of Georgia and South Carolina ever became greatly distinguished while this period was most fruitful of other great men."[6]

Waddel's democratic tendencies should not be overstated; Waddel did not make silk purses out of sows' ears at Willington. The boys he worked with had many advantages, one of which was cleverness. Good minds are a natural aristocracy, and his school specialized in nature's aristocrats. But perhaps even more important than superior mentality were character and motivation; the tortoise is said to have won over the clever hare. Even Waddel's clever boys like Calhoun, Petigru, Legare, often had the additional advantage of coming from Scotch-Irish or Huguenot homes where Calvinistic values of industry, thrift, perseverance, hard work, obedience, and respect for the written word had been drummed into their heads. In the previously mentioned case of James Louis Petigru Waddel quickly recognized the boy's creativity one day when young James interrupted a floundering story-teller and arranged the narrative in "a clear, connected manner, and in well-chosen language."[7] He then began working to persuade the family to send James to Willington. Though the details might vary, the basic fact remained: Waddel did not work to make leaders out of the featureless. In fact, he did not create leaders at all; he awakened them. Perhaps, as in the case of future college president Longstreet, he rearranged their personal values so that they could become leaders. In the case of those who came already prepared in every way but schooling, he gave the type of schooling that supposedly trained leaders, a classical education. And in fact every leader needed it, as Ramsay pointed out, to compete in the social and public life of the time.

Although Waddel had to teach classics at Willington to prepare boys for the colleges of the time and for competition with the gentlemen of Charleston, he did not teach the classics out of duty. Classical languages were his special emphasis in learning, and his love of

the classics was deep enough to inspire such students as
Hugh Swinton Legare, the grandson of Waddel's friend at
Johns Island. Hugh's father, Solomon Legare, died
young, and his widow, Mary, sent Hugh, a precocious boy,
to be schooled under the family friend, Dr. Waddel.
Even when Hugh begged to be taken out of Willington,
calling it a school of hillbillies, Mary refused stead-
fastly. Finally Hugh settled down and eventually found
Waddel's teaching on the classics so inspirational that
he went on to become a famous classicist.

    Legare, said by Parrington to have been in 1842
"perhaps the best linguist and the most widely read
man in America,"[8] wrote an essay on the benefits of
classical learning which Waddel would have applauded.
This esteemed pupil, who as Congressman and cabinet
member lived out the classic ideal, wrote in the
essay:

> All that we ask then, is, that a boy should
> be thoroughly taught the ancient languages from
> his eighth to sixteenth year, or thereabouts,
> in which time he will have his taste formed,
> his love of letters completely, perhaps enthu-
> siastically awakened, his knowledge of the
> principles of universal grammar perfected,
> his memory stored with the history, the geogra-
> phy, and the chronology of all antiquity, and
> with a vast fund of miscellaneous literature
> besides, and his imagination kindled with the
> most glorious passages of Greek and Roman poetry
> and eloquence.[9]

Legare is obviously hoping that students of the classics
will have the experience he had at Willington when Waddel
inspired his love for classical living. However, it
is simply assumed that the students will have a high
intelligence and keen imaginations and that they will
have good teachers.

    Neither Legare or Waddel would have argued for a
classical education for everyone. They both thought
in terms of their class of gentlemen or of young men
aspiring to it, of leaders, men of judgement, or plain
gentlemen. Rather like Plato in his Republic, they
were interested in studies which would serve to help
foster the production of philosopher-kings to serve as
citizen-statesmen like Legare, Calhoun, and the luminaries schooled in Waddel's academies.

    Legare said that if Americans were to study any
foreign literature at all, it ought to be classical
Greek; the reason he gave sounds like what Plato would
have used to train his high-minded citizen statesmen.
Legare says that classical civilization excelled in love

of liberty whereas modern languages were permeated with "that slavish and nauseating subserviency to rank and title, with which all European literature is steeped through and through."[10]

But the principal reason to study the classics is that Greek civilization was "the most extraordinary and brilliant phenomenon in the history of the human mind."[11] He asks why the time of a young man would not be as well spent in acquiring a knowledge of Greek as in learning algebra. His implication is that Greek is as necessary to the educated person.

Whether classical schooling, including firsthand familiarity with the great minds of ancient civilization, helped train for political prominence is questionable. But that familiarity with the Roman virtues, the history of the decline of the Roman Republic, the Athenian and Spartan civilizations, the Greek New Testament, and the great tragedies of Aeschylus, Sophocles, Euripides, must benefit a statesman and improve any person is surely unquestionable.

But in some way or other Waddel also apparently trained his future leaders to gauge the future from the facts at hand or, perhaps, how to accept intellectually facts that are not pleasing. It surely cannot be ascribed entirely to chance that all three of South Carolina's Waddel-schooled trio--Calhoun, Petigru, Legare--saw clearly the eventual ruin of the slave South. Legare said, "We are, (I am sure) the last of the race of South Carolina; I see...decay and downfall...I cherish its precious relics the more."[12] Calhoun, who saw the coming struggle and was powerless to avert it, said in 1850, "The Union is doomed to dissolution...within twelve years."[13] Petigru, the only one living at the time of secession (Calhoun had been dead for ten years, Legare for eighteen years), opposed secession because he knew it meant ruin for South Carolina.

Waddel never pretended to school the common man. As a Calvinist, Waddel worked on the assumption some were elected and set apart. Similarly at Willington he was teaching an "elect" of bright boys for social mobility and giving them the schooling he felt would raise up statesmen. His log school in the backcountry was successful in doing this. Ramsay in 1808 remarked, "Youths of great hopes are coming forward into public life from the western woods."[14]

CROMWELL OF THE CLASSROOM

Waddel spanked his students. Although some who knew him were embarrassed by the practice even then and tried to hedge when recounting it, Waddel was not in the least ashamed of it. He was a pioneer who spanked in the fight for education as naturally as others shot Indians in their fight for the frontier. And indeed violence of a sort may have been necessary. Mary Moragne, an observant novelist who knew the situation, wrote, "Boys trained to outdoor sports, and nurtured in warfare could not be easily frowned into submission, and...in the introduction of his new systems (Waddel) had many and severe contests."[1] Whether necessary or not, Waddel thought of spanking as an efficacious method of checking vice. Waddel "honestly believed that the wise suggestion of Solomon was the only safety valve for the follies of youth, and he acted upon that belief with boldness and decision."[2]

Of Waddel's moral persuasion by use of the hickory stick, Longstreet wrote "His government was one of touching 'moral suasion' but he administered it in a new way. Instead of infusing it gently into the head and heart... he applied it to the extremities, and drove it right up into the head and heart by percussion."[3] Longstreet believed that Waddel's success in turning out so many men of prominence was due to his "close vigilance" over the habits and morals of his students: "He seemed to regard vices as consuming fires and he spanked to extinguish them."[4] Longstreet further defended Waddel with the comment, "One would suppose the moral reforms so hastily produced could not last, but we have living cases to prove they have lasted for fifty-three years, and are still fresh and vigorous."[5] That argument was the clincher in that naive and pre-psychological age.

Waddel, a very pragmatic man, spanked because it worked. In fact, he believed that it sometimes worked wonders and was fond of telling of one incident to prove the point. A young man who was leaving school without paying his bills stole a horse "from some of the unsuspecting peasantry" and rode it into the heart of the Willington campus to show off. The Doctor saw him coming, hid a hickory stick inside his coat, and went out to meet him. When Waddel reached the boy on his horse, he grabbed the stirrup, pulled the boy off the horse, administered a sound thrashing, and finally told the boy he could go. However, the boy, who now wanted to stay, let the horse loose so it could go back to its barn. Not only did the boy remain but in Waddel's words, "I never had a better or more obedient pupil than he was from that day."[6] Mary Moragne, the novelist, concluded this true story by saying that "a volume might be filled with anecdotes, illustrative of his belief in the superior efficacy of coercive measures."[7]

The Doctor did, however, place some qualifications on his use of spanking. It has been mentioned that he never spanked a boy for a poorly done lesson in class. Indeed Longstreet said that in the three years he was at Willington no boy even had to do over a lesson badly done.[8] Spanking was reserved as a punishment for faulty moral conduct. Furthermore, Waddel rarely spanked in a passion or fit of temper. When he spanked a boy, Waddel was cool enough to clown or joke with him. But the only time Waddel ever actually questioned his right to beat his students was in the period of nervous collapse that went before his conversion. Then when any of his students deserved a whipping, he couldn't wholeheartedly put himself into it. Moses said he kept thinking, "If God, your great Master, would punish you for your faults, what would become of you?"[9] Here was a moment of empathy in the Gospel strain of Jesus' words "Judge not that ye be not judged" or "Blessed are the merciful." But this attitude was the product of severe depression. As soon as Waddel was "born again" religiously, he was back to beating his students without a qualm.

The fault lay probably in his Calvinistic creed. If a person were predestined, there was no free will. Without free will, no sense of tragedy developed. If there were no sense of tragedy, then understanding, empathy, and compassion did not exist. Those caught in the human tragedy learned pity. Those above it judged it, using whatever method was necessary to bring it into line. Nor was the theory of Waddel based solely on Calvinistic Christianity. "If you love them, beat them" was not far from St. Augustine's "If you love them, burn them," which was quite orthodox Christianity.

In fairness, it should be added that Waddel used spanking as a last resort. He reproved the first time, "erring the first time," as he said, "on the side of mercy."[10] But if it became evident that reproof, moral lectures, or sermons were not going to work, he whipped. It was this feeling of Christian freedom to use violence as last resort that made Waddel, "Lord Protector" of Willington, most similar to Oliver Cromwell, Lord Protector of England. Both these puritans granted a remarkable degree of freedom and justice to their citizenry. Neither used violence as a first measure, but would resort to it if all else failed. "Pray and keep the powder dry," Old Ironsides instructed his army. "Employ every possible positive teaching technique but keep the paddle handy," seems to have been Moses' view. There was in both these puritans a most unusual combination of elevated spirituality leavened with the survivor's practicality.

Cromwell had to govern England more severely than he wished because of his fear of dissident elements. Waddel had a minor if similar fear of dissident elements.

As city boys began attending more and more, the struggle
between Low Country city (Charleston) boys and up country
boys was increasingly at Willington. With too many new
students at once--and students of quite different kinds--
assimilation could not go on fast enough. Groups of new
boys fresh to the environment of Willington acted irrespon-
sibly to the point that Waddel felt they were breeding
plots and even rebellion.[11] This was around 1808. To
leave the minimum time for mischief, he made very severe
rules for a period. A horn aroused the boys at the "first
streak" of light. After breakfast, which like the other
meals lasted only fifteen minutes, the boys gathered for
prayer, and for the rest of the day were kept studying or
otherwise busy. They were even forbidden to use firearms.
How long these rules lasted is not certain, but Waddel
felt that stringent rules were necessary for a time.

The Low Country boys were dissatisfied partly because
they believed Waddel to be prejudiced against them. Since
Waddel despised the Low Country and distrusted Anglicans,
this suspicion may have been true. However, the Doctor
made a great personal effort to be impartial and was
ruthless toward any boy who suggested otherwise. When a
boy named Ned accused him of anti-Low-Country bias in
his courtroom, Waddel's face became stormy. The rare but
famed Waddel temper blew.

> He paused a second--then dropt the
> switch he had in his hand, and seizing Ned
> by all the apparel that covered his breast,
> he shook him tremendously. He lifted him
> high and sat him down emphatically, but
> not injuriously. He now waltzed him around
> the ring in the quickest possible time. He
> then made a path with him five feet deep,
> through the boys--bought him back with a
> double jerk--took another turn with him as
> before and dismissed him at the door with
> a push that sent him off at a "half hammond."
> As soon as the impetus had spent itself, Ned
> stopt, looked back, looked up, looked around
> like a man in delerium tremens, and then set
> off at a tip-toe, at a rather brisk gait,...
> and discoursing, as he went, in a sort of
> half-whisper: "The man's mad. The ma-a-ns
> mad! He made me drunk turning me around.
> If I didn't think he'd kill me, I'll never
> budge."[12]

More typical was this spanking duly administered by
Waddel after a jury verdict of guilty in the student
court. When the young man bent over, a cloth was seen
trailing out of his pants leg. Waddel tugged at the
cloth and pulled out of the boy's pants several yards of
cloth meant for padding. After the entire assembly,

including Waddel and the boy being punished, laughed, the boy was duly spanked correctly, and everyone resumed life as usual.

Waddel's belief in spanking probably simply reflected what he had learned from years of teaching experience: the desirability and even necessity of having consistent and effective punishment. The tale of the coat, which he often told, exemplified this. The boys for some passing adolescent reason came to feel that being made to take off one's coat was a serious punishment. Waddel had tried previously spanking as a last resort to stop the boys from fighting. He found he was able for the first time to stop the fighting among the boys by making a boy take off his coat in the assembly.[13] He discovered, in fact, that this "punishment" had a much better result than physical violence. However, this fact did not send him, when the coat fad passed, in search of different and possibly more effective forms of punishment. He was content to return to corporal punishment, possibly because of the scriptural blessing on spanking (such as Proverbs 13:24: "He that spareth his rod hateth his son"), which to a literal minded Calvinist settled the question.

Spanking was also a form of punishment that parents of the time expected and approved of. They were God-fearing folk who believed spanking was not simply a negative punishment but a positive good. "Raise them on a Bible and a hickory stick," was a frontier saying. The boys were so accustomed to spanking at home that they did not resent Waddel's punishing them in this manner. If anything, a spanking with a hickory stick increased his caring paternal image because it was exactly what their fathers would have done when they misbehaved. The fathers equally expected Dr. Waddel to stand in loco parentis and do his moral duty by spanking when a boy offended.

In fairness, it should be added that spanking was only a duty; he did not particularly enjoy it. He was a practical Christian who reviewed his motivations constantly in sweet Calvinistic agony. It was probably partially because of this sensitivity to his own motives that he refused to spank in anger or passion, unless it was one of those occasions, rare but memorable, his temper carried him away. He did not wish to become accustomed to the satisfaction of passion through beating. To picture him as a sadist enjoying spanking is to buy melodrama at the expense of truth. The evidence is that Waddel was neither a pervert nor a fiend. He was a good man, a hero to many boys, but a hero with a paddle rather than a six-gun.

Calvinism has a very literal view of the Kingdom of God. Although the New Testament comments that the Kingdom of God cannot be taken by violence, Calvinists, like Moslems, have never accepted this. After all, the

Moslems, who converted a large part of the Christian world by force, found that violence did, to a degree, work. Even to Calvinists, however, violence was not a cure-all but a last resort which often worked or helped. It would have been absolutely useless to ask the Rev. Dr. Hall not to march off to the American Revolution with the men of his congregation armed to kill the British, to ask Oliver Cromwell not to lead his army against Charles I, or to ask Moses Waddel to stop spanking boys when they broke rules of moral conduct. John Knox's preaching of the divine right of rebellion against unjust rulers and his appeal to violence as the last resort of the elect endured as an important part of Calvinism.

Far from believing in spanking as a cure-all, Waddel believed that the basic problem, human nature and original sin, was resolvable not by earthly means, but only by divine grace. But violence could keep things under control. As Alexander Hamilton had seen at seventeen, "a vast majority of mankind is entirely biased by motives of self-interest." If mankind learned that punishment was swift, then it would be in their self-interest not to commit anti-social acts, and they might not do it.

After Waddel set up his court and jury system at Willington and saw it working, he brought his use of violence inside the law. Finally he spanked only upon the verdict of a jury who knew the law. Eventually corporal punishment even by the court was rarely inflicted though not wholly excluded.[14] These were great steps in an age when schoolmasters ruled very often like barbarians and madmen, as "those without the law."

But it was Waddel's "boldness and decision" on punishment that made him one of the great puritans. He realized that, whatever positive inducements might be offered (and he offered many), there was a definite need for serious and consistent punishment at times. He was not afraid to employ it. Although a man prone to nervous collapses, he found in his faith the "iron nerve and unbending resolution"[15] to fully exercise his power in order that boys might learn in an orderly atmosphere conducive to learning.

COMMENCEMENT AND COLLEGE

At the first commencement of South Carolina College in 1807 Moses Waddel was awarded the honorary title of Doctor of Divinity,[1] along with three other clergymen, one Anglican, one Baptist and another Presbyterian. On January 18, 1806, Jonathan Maxcy, first President of South Carolina College, wrote Waddel that the education of youth was of vast importance to society, "especially under such a free and excellent government as is ours" and that he hoped he had the "kind offices of the friends of religion and learning of all denominations."[2] Granting degrees to distinguished clergymen of different denominations was certainly one way to get them.

"Kind offices" could have been interpreted as "students." The degree, in truth, was a device to persuade Waddel to send students to the college. And the students were needed: in the letter Maxcy said the college had two professors and fifty-one students. Waddel alone had around 180 at Willington. Since few from the Low Country were students at the time,[3] the college desperately needed to get students from Piedmont academies such as Willington. This need was made plain to Willington boys. Jones, a student at South Carolina College, included this dialogue in a letter to Waddel dated January 11, 1806:

> It was hinted to me by one of the faculty that he understood the greater part of your students graduated from Princeton College, and seemed surprised that so few come to this place.
>
> I told him that those who wished to graduate northerly, you generally recommended to Princeton, but it was altogether owing to the choice of the student.
>
> He asked me if any more of your students intended coming here? I told him it was quite probable.[4]

South Carolina College eventually became a favorite college for students from Willington to attend. James Louis Petigru, Hugh Swinton Legare, and George McDuffie were among the most prominent who went there from Willington.

Commencements were always a grand affair, whether at college or at the academy. Willington's commencement, in fact, continued several days and was attended by large crowds. The outline of the program was described by Longstreet. First there was the examination of all the classes by prominent visitors. When John C. Calhoun examined them in 1807, he wrote home to Florida, "Not long since I attended an examination at Mr. Waddel's with which I was much pleased, as the students appeared generally correct and well informed."[5] Examiners usually asked students to translate and analyze passages of Latin or Greek. Next was oratory, for which prizes were awarded, and finally the performance of one or two dramatic pieces, usually a comedy and farce: "The speakers were divided into three classes, according to their age and advancement; the first class being composed generally of the oldest students in the school; the second, of those next in years; and the third, or the youngest excluding those in the elementary studies."[6] The exhibition of October 19, 1797, offered two plays and at least twelve speeches, one of which was "The Death of Washington."

A rough stage of log planks was placed in front of the main entrance to the school, and the front door of the school was in the center of the stage. On this stage sat the examiners and judges, along with Dr. Waddel and chosen speakers from the student body. The platform and speakers were shaded by "stately oaks." Although examinations did not begin until nine in the morning, the visitors started arriving at seven: "People of all ranks, ages, sexes and sizes might be seen wending their way to the school house, or rather to the area in front of it."[7] Although the boys' dress was usually drab because Waddel's dress code forbade expensive clothes and encouraged homespun to foster democracy at the school, on this one day the boys were decked out in turkey red, indigo blue, nankeen, and gingham.

After commencement came college, where newcomers would take the critical test to determine whether they had enough knowledge to be placed in the junior class. In a letter of May 1, 1803, to Dr. Waddel John W. Walker, an alumnus, tells about taking the critical test that enabled him to enter the junior class. In the next section he gives, in reply to Waddel's questions, some idea of the daily schedule.

> When we entered he (the Rev. Dr. Samuel S. Smith, President of Princeton) was in his closet but soon came out and was presented with our letters from Waddel, which he read in the order they were written. When he finished the perusal of mine he made some few inquiries concerning my studies, promising that you had expressed a desire for my admission into the junior (class).

> Such answers were returned as were thought necessary--nearly correspondent with your assertions. After going through the whole he conducted us unto Dr. Hunter, the professor of Mathematics, with whom he left Mr. Posey and myself, taking Willis with himself to Mr. Thompson, the professor of languages. Mr.

Hunter perused our credentials too, of chemistry and Natural Philosophy, stepped in, to whom I then delivered a letter which had been written in my favor by his quondam class mate, Doctor Murray of Augusta.

Monday being appointed for our examination, we that day hastened to meet our fate. By Mr. Maclean we were made known to Mr. Thompson and after a desultory conversation of a quarter of an hour, we entered the house which contains the library.

Here Virgil and Horace and Lucian and Zenophon and Mair* were successively opened to us. After we had read the necessary quantities in each, we were informed that "we were admitted into the Junior Class but must make up those studies in which we were deficient." We can be examined in geography and Kennett when we pleased, and we think of demanding an audience at an early period after commencement of next session. Algebra, Euclid and the Sunday lectures must for some time employ our attention, and these we must make up and a part of Trigonometry too, and at the same time keep pace with our class. There are square and cube root, which will be an additional burden on my poor shoulders, the weight of which Brookes will not feel, as he is extremely well versed in them. Thus, you see, my dear sir, our hands will be full and we must burn the taper of midnight frequently....

You will observe Homer is not mentioned in the number of those authors on whom we were tested. This happened because there was no book of that kind by. This we regretted greatly in as much as we flattered ourselves with the belief we could have translated him with greater ease than any of the others-- Apropos--but one book of Homer is read here by the sophomores, whereas you read twelve.[8]

(In a letter of June 15, 1803 he gives, in answer to Waddel's questions, some idea of the daily schedule.)

A college bell rings at half past five a.m. and as its noise is not deemed sufficient for the two lower entries, one of the servants blows a trumpet from end to end in the passage....

---

*Mair's Introduction, a Latin text.

At six the bell is tolled a second time which is the signal for prayers. All meet in a room appropriated to that...use, when one of our two tutors offers the appropriate morning sacrifice....

A chapter from the Bible is constantly read in the morning. After prayer all retire to study until half past seven when the breakfast horn is blown. From that hour till nine is allowed for relaxation.

At nine the bell rings again when the Sophomore and Freshman classes repair to their separate recitation rooms where they remain till twelve. At eleven the first division of the Senior class recites and the second at two. We have, however, today adopted another hour--first division at ten a.m.--second division at eleven a.m.

This is when we recite to Dr. Hunter-- two days in the week, to Doctor Maclean three days in the week, and to Doctor Smith one day.

On Sunday the Junior class recites at four p.m. theological lectures by Henry Hollock, the Seniors those lectures written by Dr. Smith, the sophomore classes on the evidence of the Christian religion from a printed pamphlet and the freshman the catechism of the denomination of their choice. From ten to one we have play time.

At one dinner is served up. The room is large, eight tables and all full. One of the professors is obliged by the duties of his office to attend and eat in the refectory one week in rotation. The Senior class goes in first, the rest in order. All standing up, the tutor says grace, and they they fall to work pass the bread-- Hughey, butter--Peter, milk--Simon, coffee-- Isaac, potatoes--gravy--bread--bread, bread, resound from a hundred mouths.

In retiring from dinner, which is far from being luxurious, they push each other unmercifully.

At five the bell rings, all meet, the roll is called. Doctor Smith delivers evening prayers and the orators mount the stage--three orators each night. All then disperse...to supper....

Instead of teas or coffee at supper nothing but milk and bread, but at breakfast we have coffee and butter. Then we have till nine at night hours for relaxation. Then the tutor comes to every room to see if inmates play truant. Then to bed as soon as you please. Thus you have one day. All are alike except on Sunday we go to church and have a piece of pie for dinner!

John B. Posey wrote Doctor Waddel from Princeton in 1805, "The Southern students stand very high here, more so than others. They are a little dissipated which comes from their possessing too much cash."[9] Dr. Waddel in the same year sent Posey a list of "serious hints," on what subjects we do not know. Posey wrote back to Dr. Waddel, "Be assured that your 'serious hints' were taken kindly and persued with pleasure."[10] Dr. Waddel's genuine interest in his students did not stop when they left him. The old puritan advised on.

No doubt his students, such as Posey, were amused by him at times. In one letter John Posey wrote he had been to a theatre, then, remembering, apologized, "I forgot that you hate the theatre."[11] But in spite of their amusement they knew his interest in their success was sincere. This may have been one reason so many of Waddel's students remembered him and his school so fondly.

DECISIONS, DECISIONS

In 1818 Waddel, the teacher "whose real function on earth was surely the teaching of boys," was once again "hankering after a pulpit"[1] and had turned the school and his teaching at Willington over to an assistant. Waddel was planning to spread the gospel full time on an evangelistic tour of the backwoods.

A preoccupation with religion on a full-time basis usually meant that Waddel was having trouble with his "nerves." Dr. Alonzo Church expressed politely this side of Waddel when he said in a eulogy, "he had not what the world calls the strongest nerves."[2] Waddel had become obsessed with religion and given up teaching after the first serious depression and nervous breakdown that preceded his conversion. Later he closed his academy and gave himself to religious evangelism after his first wife died and he had another breakdown.

In one sense, of course, he had always put his church first. He had moved the location of the best academy in the South, maybe in the nation, several times as he moved from one tiny part-time congregation to the next. Although the top enrollment of his academy was as large as his biggest congregation, he dragged his boys after him, placing the spiritual welfare of small rural congregations of drab and relentlessly respectable Presbyterians before the future of an academy that was early turning out great leaders.

Waddel saw the goal of education as a chance to inculcate truth,[3] by which he meant ultimately Christianity. In the New Testament, truth implied a relationship with God; to have this relationship was to have truth. Jesus called Himself "the way, the truth and the light" in John 14:6. Waddel was a Christian propagandist to whom the virtue of his students was more important than their learning and the morality of a teacher was more important that intellectuality or brilliance. In fact, in this light it is ironic that his academies turned out so many prominent politicians. It hints of Goethe's comment on Napoleon that he started out to find virtue, but since it was unobtainable, settled for power.

In 1818 Waddel had given up the teaching, the last thing he should have given up, and was devoting himself full time to his religious duties, the first thing he should have given up. To be fair to Waddel, it should be noted that the amount of work involved in doing two jobs as punctually and thoroughly as he did them resulted in an extremely heavy work schedule. To accomplish it he had to rise with the dawn in summer and before dawn in winter all his life.[4] Wanting to give up one was natural, and to him the logical one to give up was teaching. Why go through all that teaching demanded in order to bring a few young people to truth, i.e., Jesus and virtue, when simple preaching could bring more? At the Lexington, Kentucky camp meeting in 1801 six thousand attended, three hundred joined the church, and seventy were struck with the conviction of sin.[5] Education was fine, but evangelism was quicker.

As the Reverend Dr. Waddel was preparing to leave on a personal evangelism tour, the call to the Presidency of the University of Georgia came. The call caused his third nervous breakdown, in which he went into a depression and spent much time in prayer. His son said, "the mental conflicts through which he passed in the consideration and decision of this question were extremely distressing."[6] For a time it seemed as though the depression "would prove disastrous." A friend said that when Waddel was considering the question posed by the University of Georgia, his sufferings were "extreme" and his mental anxiety was "deep."[7] Finally came the feeling of peace, which he interpreted as a divine communication, one of the definite "impressions" from God which he always believed he had. He was now sure that accepting the presidency was "clearly his duty"; the will of God was pointing out to him what he should do."[8] Out of his subconscious the feeling that he was awaiting came as he prayed.

Dr. Church, a friend of Waddel's at Athens and later President of the University of Georgia, says that Waddel made many decisions in this way. Through agonizing prayer "in all the business of life"[9] he tried to find the will of God. When he received a certain impression which he attributed to God, that decided the issue. For example, President Waddel, after much discussion with the faculty, decided on a particular policy, which he was to announce at evening prayers in the chapel. Before chapel "Dr. Waddel was as decided in his opinion as any," but when he entered the chapel, "a doubt came into his mind" and during evening prayers he "prayed most earnestly." Instead of announcing the policy, he left the chapel without telling anyone anything. After he had prayed some more and his mind had searched the matter, he informed Dr. Church that the new policy was cancelled because of "an intimation from the Spirit of God."[10] Dr. Church wisely commented, "whatever influence controlled his mind," events proved that it was the right course. Later on it was found that if the new policy had been implemented, "probably melancholy consequences would have ensued." All were unaware of these possible consequences at the time.

Although Dr. Waddel's communication system with God was more subtle than the voices of Joan of Arc, there can be no doubt that Dr. Waddel believed himself to be in direct communication with God, to be a receiver through his subconscious of intimations from God that directed him. Since furthermore he strove for these intimations often in prayer, it was small wonder he was a case of nerves. His decisions were never reached in the clear light of logical day, but rather at night in an agony of religious suffering over questions at hand until a certain mystical feeling, "an intimation of God," appeared to match the issue. When that feeling of psychological security blessed one side or the other of an issue, then that side was the will of God. After Waddel believed it was the will of God, his attitude was "do or die," for his most personal text or motto was the fiercely independent words of the Apostle Paul: "I am chargeable to no man" (2 Corinthians 11:9).[11]

Although Waddel's decisions were deeply intuitive, however, they were contained within prescribed social limits set down by church and custom. In this way he was able to be a respectable Christian gentleman of his time, yet dare to be intuitive, different and nonconforming on methods, techniques, and minor decisions on his school and students. Never, for example, would he have asked spiritual direction on obedience to blue laws, Sabbath restrictions, and pietistic living. These were handed down in the Bliblical divine guidebook by God Almighty to Calvinists and were beyond questioning. Prayer and soul searching were done only within a rigidly prescribed set of moral rules. One might pray over how to implement the rule or pray for grace to observe it, but never about the rule itself.

The fact that Waddel was morally compulsive, somewhat cold, terrified of losing his self-control, accounts for the depressions and breakdowns he suffered when faced with change or insecurity. When insecurity faced him, he went into severe depressions until through prayer he could come up with a God-given security. The idea behind the folk truth, "Man proposes, God laughs," was completely foreign to him. Waddel did not doubt for a moment that when he prayed, God listened.

Whenever anything awful happened, when Waddel found himself disobeying his father as a boy, or his wife died, or his job appeared to change, Waddel broke down. He worked himself back to security through prayer as God gave him intimations on how to proceed. Whatever may be the reason Dr. Waddel prayed, he received some very interesting answers. Furthermore, prayer sharpened his intuition and gave the quality of the unexpected to what otherwise might have been a dismal, boring, and too respectable Calvinist life.

Once Waddel had reached a decision through mysterious fishings in subconscious seas, however, he had to give a logical reason--possibly, to paraphrase Milton, to justify the ways of God to Waddel. He told his son, John, that he accepted the Presidency of Franklin College to elevate the college to a position of usefulness in Georgia. His other reason was that he wished to endow public education with the spirit of Christianity.[12] In fact, he said that he accepted only after he found he could preach regularly in the college chapel.[13]

His first two reasons were exactly what he had learned at college. It was the rare ecumenical vision that founded Hampden-Sydney as a nondenominational school involving different faiths to serve the total community--"to form good men and good citizens on the common and universal principles of morality."[14] Here was Calvinism in an elevated and socially healthy state freed from the literalisms of Geneva, the legalisms of Levitical law, and self-serving denominational interests. It was the Calvinistic social conscience giving brotherly service even to the gross and unelect under a common heaven. (There is no way to know whether these were his true reasons. Waddel was a mystic desperately seeking to discern the will of God so that the elect could carry it out. The reasons for a mystic's decisions are not clear.)

Waddel's emphasis on intuitiveness and emotionalism in religion was a reaction to 18th century "deism" with its emphasis on reason and logic. Longstreet emphasized in Waddel's funeral eulogy that his religion was part of the reaction against the "enlightenment" and the liberal excesses of the French Revolution. Longstreet said, "Dr. Waddel's character, will be considered as overdrawn by those...who do not contemplate it with reverence to the age in which he lived. It was emphatically the infidel age of the world.... Montesquieu...Voltaire...Diderot and D'Alembert...this glittering host were...taking the souls of men, and leading them to ruin.... It was at this time..'that Moses Waddel...entered Hampden-Sydney College. He lived to see the principles of these brilliant reformers, in full operation. France convulsed and frenzied, disgorging blood at every spasm.... The Marseillaise hymn reverberating through the streets of Paris...Robespierre, Marat and Danton, unkenneled."[15]

Reason, logic, and rationality--the "enlightenment" qualities--had ended in the frenzy of the French Revolution and the dictatorship of Napoleon. Waddel, along with many others, turned to emotionalism, revivalism, and mysticism in religion and conservatism in morality in reaction to the failure of reason and logic. In a different type of turning away Emerson and Thoreau reacted to deism with a transcendentalism that stressed the value of intuition and mystical oneness with the "over-soul."

It was probably lucky for Old Moses that this stream of colorful irrationality was introduced into what otherwise was a narrow life. The compulsive person like Waddel has "an exaggerated sense of responsibility" and an "excessive need for perfection." He has a hard time making up his mind, "but once he decides...he holds stubbornly to it. He is almost totally incapable of relaxing and usually has an earnest, driven, humourless air." Compulsive people express hostility by "dominating others and holding them to lofty standards. At the same time they may hold themselves to high standards as a safeguard against aggressive impulses or feelings of guilt which often date back to childhood with overcritical parents.... Not surprisingly, if a psychological disorder does develop, it usually takes the form of obsessive compulsive neurosis."[16]

Waddel, who felt a responsibility to save large areas from hell, was constantly going out to hold evangelistic crusades. He exhibited a perhaps excessive need for perfection by holding all the tedious Calvinistic blue laws. He had a breakdown when he had to make up his mind. As for relaxing, Longstreet described him as an "engine." He dominated his students and held the very highest standards, holding the "faith and the dogmas of his church in their straightest and strictest forms,"[17] as a possible safeguard against the feelings of guilt caused by his overly pious parents. In his most explicitly described breakdown preceding his conversion, he showed obsessive compulsive symptoms.

After Waddel made up his mind to go to Franklin College, the matter was over because God had revealed Himself. After going up to look over the situation and to serve as president for a semester, Waddel returned to Willington where he wrote John C. Calhoun on December 19, 1819:

> On the 19th ult(im)o I arrived here with my family in order to spend the vacation, attend to the sale of my Cotton-crop and prepare for a removal of my furniture etc. to Athens....
>
> I am informed that the General Government supports a number of youths at West Point as Cadets in the Military School with an allowance.... I am led earnestly to solicit your friendship to be exercised in behalf of a youth of Elbert County.... He is said...to possess Intellect in an unusual degree.... He is about entering his seventeenth year and is an Orphan....
>
> I hope, if spared, to set out for Athens with my family and about half of my hands on next Tuesday (the 21st). After my arrival and settlement there, I shall be glad to drop you a line and hear from you when agreeable and convenient. You never have informed me whether you asked the President (James Munroe) how he liked his reception at Athens...this

day rec(eive)d his Message from Mr. (Thomas W.) Cobb, Representative from (Georgia). I am very sorry to observe one important defect in it, vis. no intimation or acknowledgement of national dependence on or obligation to Divine Providence."[18]

Waddel was not such a rare type. New England had been full of these compulsive and mystical Puritans for years. However, Waddel was a landmark for the University of Georgia as its first Southern-born and Southern-educated president.

THE UNIVERSITY OF GEORGIA

"Success to the University of Georgia," President Monroe toasted in 1819 to a dinner party given in his honor at Athens.[1] Seated at the table with Monroe was Moses Waddel, the new president of that institution, and the man upon whom success depended. Earlier in the day Waddel had conducted Monroe to his hotel and made a speech of welcome to him. That night a dinner party was given Monroe, and the college held a festival "illumination" or lighting of all rooms in the college buildings. This had been the fashion since the illumination of all Paris on the night of Napoleon's wedding to Marie Louise.

Had the students and town of Athens been wiser, they might have rejoiced over the arrival of Moses Waddel, the new president of the University, rather than a passing tourist President of the United States. The former came to accomplish and put down roots. The latter was one more celebrity passing through. Nor was "success" the right term to toast the University of Georgia with at the time. "Survival" was a better word.

Waddel's earliest contact with the University of Georgia came in 1799 when the Senatus Academicus, the governing body of what was to be the University of Georgia, made a futile attempt to name Waddel's Academy in Columbia County the University of Georgia. When other counties became envious and nominated their own academies (if they had one), the Senatus Academicus despairingly adjourned until 1800.[2] Had Waddel's Academy been designated the University of Georgia in 1799, the college could have saved itself an unusual career of early bumbling, although the greatest academy in the South would never have been born. As things turned out, when Waddel went to the University, his work was far harder than a founder's because he had to push uphill against a bad reputation.

The college had one thing in its favor: with an income of $8,000 a year from the state plus the tuition of the students[3] and with the buildings paid for, it had no urgent financial problems. Of course, since there were only four, including Waddel, on the faculty in 1819, and Waddel's salary, the highest, was $2200 a year, it was relatively easy to make ends meet. And although Waddel was undeniably lucky not to have a pressing economic problem, this was the only way in which the college was fortunate.

After Waddel's death A. B. Longstreet wrote, "The success which attended his efforts in raising the institution so rapidly as he did to respectability, has been to many inexplicable. But to those who well understood his character that success is by no means surprising."[4]

81

But "character" is too vague a word. He was honest, of course, but many unsuccessful college presidents are. To begin with, he brought a famous name with him. Furthermore, an examination of his diary shows that he diligently raised academic standards, promoted good public relations, proclaimed a moral atmosphere, and made himself constantly visible and accessible to students. All these factors together made his success. The idea that he accomplished a miracle on "character" is misleading.

The first factor, the famous name that he brought, was partly the result of luck in that some of Waddel's students, especially Crawford and Calhoun, had risen to prominence quickly and on a national scale. These students, often remembering Waddel fondly and feeling grateful to him, encouraged his educational efforts. Calhoun and Crawford were among Waddel's alumni who came back to his school on great occasions, maintained relations with him, and publicized his abilities. Nor was Waddel an insignificant public relations man himself. In <u>College Life in the Old South</u> E. M. Coulter remarked on Waddel's fame in 1819, "Ever since the age of fourteen (1784) he had been busily teaching and preaching himself into a fame that had by this time spread over the whole Southeast."[5]

When a friend in Athens complimented Dr. Waddel on his administrative diligence, it was a fairly earned compliment. It was a rare day as head of the college that he did not examine a class. This constant examination helped keep interest focused on studies and helped maintain high academic standards, which meant a growing reputation and a pride in the school. His diary of March 28, 1836 showed that in one day he examined classes on logic, natural philosophy, Euclid, Homer, and geography. More significantly, when he found the examination of the senior class to be deficient, he made fifteen students repeat the examination. In a school whose total enrollment was not much above one hundred, deferring fifteen seniors was a daring step. However, it was necessary to re-establish standards and pride. Sometimes he went so far as to send for students who were doing poorly in their studies and talk to them. Of course, this fatherly approach did not always work. His diary records that when he sent for Albert Simmons and "spoke to him about his studies," young Simmons was offended.

Waddel's presence at the college guaranteed the moral atmosphere that was necessary if respectable parents were to feel free to send their sons there. However, the moral atmosphere usually took the form of too many trivial rules. In this time a college was more like a preparatory school, where the administration was expected to keep a close watch on the boys. Waddel did little about the rules except to create more. To the school's already existing rules he added prohibitions against novels and dancing. (Fortunately there were no theatres very close.) Although it would have been unthinkable public relations in that morally strict era to abolish rules, Waddel need not have added more. Common offenses at the college were swearing, promoting cockfights, idleness, drinking, gambling (especially card-playing), and disrespect to professors. A great deal of time and energy was spent yearly on punishing these. While the faculty was seeking to socialize the students and to make them obey rules, the students often felt themselves to be outgrowing rules. Clashes were inevitable.

Waddel succeeded in making his own life very uncomfortable by having all these rules. His diary would record that he heard a "french horn" in the night, a violation of the curfew and the noise rules. But it was not simply one horn. By the end of his presidency he seems to have heard an entire band. After each offense that occurred in the night he rose the next day to find the offender. Predictably he rarely did. Almost incredibly, he never seems to have realized that the students were playing cat and mouse with him. Since he saw the punishment of offenders as his duty, he continued to play the game which he did not recognize as such. He was a terribly literal man and far too earnest to see the humor of the situation. But the picture is clear: shortly after he douses the light in his room and crawls in his high bedstead, comes the sound of a French horn carefully planted nearly within range of the old man's hearing. Later it will be a trumpet. The president lies there, noting that he must check into it tomorrow. The whole episode is a scene from opera bouffe, but scrupulous, humorless Waddel was constitutionally unable to stop being irritated, and boys being boys, once the students grasped this, they were unable to give up the sport of irritating him--and interfering with his sleep. He recorded in his diary, Wednesday, March 17, 1824--"awoke not refreshed by sleep, having been interrupted by a disorderly company in the night, who had music round the house."

In the boys' defense, it should be noted that Waddel did a lot of useless irritating of the students. For example, he used a telescope to spy the horizon to try to find boys sneaking off to Witter's drinking house.[6] When he spied some, he went after them and marched them back. Did he spank offenders? Moses' son, John, said that he did not. Waddel scolded boys for use of ugly language and sometimes acted as trustee for the parents and doled out pocket money. But he did not spank. Disciplinary matters came up before the president and faculty, who could vote to expel and often did.

How these boys were strong enough to stay up nights to carouse--or to tease Dr. Waddel--is remarkable itself when one considers that they had classes before breakfast. It was an unbelievable spasm of leniency for the administration in 1828 to stop holding classes before breakfast on Monday morning. When Dr. Waddel made this surprisingly uncharacteristic concession to the hangover, the issue was no doubt presented to him in other terms.

·The way Waddel handled the moral image of the campus was to maintain for show a great many paper rules which were enforced if the offender could be caught. The students' dislike of rules in general and their utter contempt for many of them was simply ignored. Equipped with paper rules, an occasional act of justice, and a refusal to admit that anything was wrong, Waddel fooled the public well. Indeed in his public statements the old puritan was not above stretching the truth in order to have a good image. Coulter points out that in 1824 when the students at the University were "particularly unruly," Dr. Waddel declared that they showed "respectful submission to the laws."[7] One can sympathize with Waddel or any administrator. Telling the truth about campus discipline would have caused a crisis which would have ruined the already weakened college. Waddel, like any successful clergyman, ignored reality and went full steam ahead. It was by far the wisest thing to do.

The earnest image of Dr. Waddel himself was an asset. A pious Georgia mother might have no fear in sending her son to study under so Christian a man in (if the rule book could be believed) such an oppressively moral atmosphere. At the same time the students, as normal and healthy adolescents, continued doing what students have always done. The situation was a standoff in which the status quo was preserved. Nobody was happy but nobody was too unhappy. It was the normal stalemate of life.

Waddel also was careful to foster public relations by paying attention to the parents of the students. His diary shows that he regularly received parents, talked to them, and wrote to them about the performance of their sons. If a father wished to come to the school to see for himself the progress of his boy, then Waddel arranged examinations in academic subjects by the faculty before the father. An example of this is recorded in Waddel's diary for August 20, 1825: "Examined John Heard with faculty in my room--wrote fully to his brother, Franklin." He wrote on another day, "Called on William R. and Sam Brown's--He went with me to my college room and faculty met to examine his sons."

By this time the question and answer instinct had become second nature to Dr. Waddel. Once when a guest preacher in chapel began shouting Luke 10:13 ("Woe unto thee, Chorazin! woe unto thee, Bethsaida! for if the mighty works had been done in Tyre and Dison which have been done in you, they had...repented"), he shouted, "Woe unto thee," and forgot the rest. In the embarrassing silence Waddel instinctively prompted the preacher full voice as he had prompted so many students: "Chorazin." The effect, it was said, was "starting." But it got the preacher back on the track, and the sermon was finished happily and uneventfully.[8]

Visibility was one secret of Waddel's administrative success. Various contemporary studies have demonstrated that visibility, the quality of being accessible and seen much, is one of the characteristics of the successful administrator. Dr. Waddel was nothing if not visible to both the town and the campus. His diary shows that he attended regularly every campus event unless he felt very unwell. He attended what must have been every community gathering in the village of Athens as well as his church meetings. His diary pages exhibit a compulsive list of events, debates, Bible societies, faculty college parties, and lectures that made heavy inroads into his time. Surprisingly he showed he had the temperament of a successful clubman who did not mind going in the least. And even upon his return home in the evening he was always delighted to find someone else to visit or talk to. His friends thought nothing of coming for a talk until bedtime; Waddel thought nothing at all of calling on others at breakfast, though he did note when his host did not offer him any eggs. Athens brought him out socially.

Rural dwellers, customarily starved for society, rarely get to see enough of people and are delighted to have them around. It is plain Waddel, after his years at Willington, enjoyed life in a town, even a very small one. Ordinary townspeople were flattered by his presidential presence. When he was taken quite sick for several days, he recorded in his diary very proudly that nearly "every respectable person" in the village came to see him. How he stood the visiting, as sick as he was, remains a question.

Waddel's sociability, church involvement, campus event attendance, and class examinations gave him the visibility that a successful administrator needs. He did appear in all places and was accessible to all sorts of students and citizens. There is little doubt he knew by name most people on the campus and in the town--no remarkable feat of memory, in view of the smallness of both, but still a remarkable proof of involvement. It gave him some good entrees: "Today saw old Mr. Rosencaval in street and asked him if he had joined any church," he records in his diary. He always thought of his church as well as the college.

Since there were no college sports at the time, debating served an important social function very much like football rallies. Waddel was always present; indeed, knowing the heat some topics generated, he was probably afraid to be absent. One diary entry, for example, records that he heard "seniors on adultery," and he also heard speeches on such political issues as the merits of aristocracy versus democracy and even the abolition of slavery. He apparently did not like some things he heard, and said so. On one occasion he heard the remarks of the evening, then got up and made a typical Waddelian speech on morality. On another occasion for moral discussion Waddel noted in his diary on March 24, 1829 that he spoke to "the girls" (probably a female academy) about "bad women."

It was said that Waddel did not restructure Franklin College along some of the brilliant and progressive lines he had used at Willington. He did not for a variety of reasons.

To begin with, he was called to save the college and not restructure it. A more important reason is that the collge was a state-owned institution and he did not have freedom to do as he liked. Under state direction the college was striving, like most provincial colleges, not to be original, but to succeed by being a cheaper imitation of longer established and more sophisticated colleges such as Yale. That such a policy condemned it to second rateness was not considered relevant at the time.

In fact, it is not clear whether Waddel ever even knew what he had created at Willington and why. He knew of course that he had done something extraordinary, but it is very doubtful that he saw Willington as an integrated structure of balanced techniques and methods. Not being a systematic thinker, Waddel did not start from a vision and create; his structure was the result of piecemeal intuitions. It is probable he never appreciated Willington as an architectonic conception capable of benefiting schools elsewhere.

Waddel, obsessed with Christianity, spent his time trying to imbue students with the spirit of Christianity through sermons, a highly doubtful procedure, rather than spending his time on the consideration of the basic structure of institutional life. This misplaced emphasis was his tragedy, because the reason students did not listen to his moral lectures and sermons as they might have, lay really in their response to the way their life was structured. Treated as incompetents in a dictatorial system, they responded as bottom groups will--by apathy, laziness, indifference, and living for the joy of the moment.

Eventually various people began seeking to oust him. In 1824 after the college was flourishing again, "one or two of the trustees thinking that Dr. Waddel had done all the good he was fitted to perform," asked him to resign, because they wanted "one of more distinguished literary reputation." This reaction was usual academic snobbery: Waddel had been in secondary school education and was thus not fit to be at college level.

There was also the problem created by the envy of other denominations who resented the heavy Presbyterian influence at the state-supported college. Since the Methodists and Baptists did not demand an educated ministry, while the Presbyterians did, the Presbyterian ministry almost inevitably played a larger role than their numbers would warrant in the intellectual life of many Southern colleges. Members of other denominations, seeing only the denomination and forgetting the qualifications, objected. Waddel was subjected to a heavy amount of anti-Presbyterian sentiment. These put pressure on him to resign to weaken the Presbyterian influence at the college. So Dr. Waddel resigned.

Although Waddel was, in fact, only too happy to seize an opportunity to resign that he might go about full-time preaching, his departure would have been unfortunate. Waddel had unquestionably revived the college, but its reputation still rested on him. More time was needed to accustom people to thinking of the college as a good school in its own right. As it was, popular opinion considered it a coming school solely because Waddel was there.

After Waddel's tendered resignation passed the college board of trustees, it was sent to be approved by the higher educational governing board of Georgia, The Senatus Academicus. One member was a Willington alumnus, George Gilmer, who had been part of the commission sent to the college to plead with Dr. Waddel to accept the presidency. Gilmer of course did not want Waddel to leave the college. When the resignation was before the Senatus Academicus, Gilmer presented a resolution asking Dr. Waddel to stay on as president and another one expressing "high appreciation" of Waddel's value and his contributions to the college. The resolution passed almost unanimously. Gilmer wrote in his memoirs that he did not believe "any act of my after life was more cordially approved by the people of Georgia"[9] (a strong statement since he was elected governor twice and a congressman three times).

Of course some animosity remained even after the "vote of confidence." On December 31, 1824 Waddel recorded-- "met three trustees at noon in the old chapel--one of them retired abruptly with hurt feelings.... Reflected seriously on the close of the year 1824." Nonetheless "Old Moses" stayed on at the college until 1829. Grasping the use of approbation, the Senatus Academicus and college trustees sang his praises regularly. Waddel would not leave as long as he felt he was successfully accomplishing his Christian mission to put the college on its feet and imbue it with the spirit of Christianity. After all, Waddel's decision to go to the University of Georgia supposedly had been for purposes of Christian service to the community and to some extent an act of Christian charity. After it was obvious that the school was on its feet, Waddel felt his work was done, as indeed it was, and he showed an interest in returning to Willington, which he considered his home. Characteristically his consideration was not money but preaching time. He wished to do more preaching, as he always had. But he could leave the college stable now. The year was 1829.

Waddel brought to the University of Georgia not only high-toned (if narrow) Christianity but also a remarkable grasp of the practical qualities needed by a successful administrator. This fortunate practical union of Christian social conscience with diligence and common sense was distinctly puritan. The University of Georgia was extremely fortunate that in its hour of crisis, there appeared a competent and efficient executive with a social conscience. In any age, these are rare men. As to the minor eccentricities these men have, one must do as Waddel himself did on occasion, ignore certain aspects of reality in everybody's best interests and keep going.

Yet it was a relief when he left. The students no longer had to go behind trees to try to avoid the telescope of Dr. Waddel peering out to see who went to drinking houses. Novels came out from under mattresses to reappear respectably on the shelves. Dancing, which had gone underground, commenced again legitimately. When Waddel left, in fact, it soon reappeared publicly in its most gala form, a commencement ball in 1830. And while the sneaking during Waddel's tenure was all absolutely comic, it was a small enough price in forebearance to pay for the services of the old puritan. For if any man ever saved a college, it was this fifth President of the University of Georgia.

The most famous student of Waddel's at Franklin College, Alexander Hamilton Stephens, future Vice-President of the Confederacy, said of Waddel later: "In his insight into the character of boys, the constitution of their minds, their capacities and attitudes, and in drawing out and developing their faculties by proper training, discipline and government, he had few, if any, superiors in the United States."[10]

But perhaps the best resumé of Waddel's contribution, though obviously a biased one, is in Waddel's letter to a state historian, Joseph V. Bevan, written apparently in 1829-30 but dated March 14, 1825.[11] In it Waddel gave a detailed review of progress he had made but did not tell, and probably did not know, how he made it.

Athers, 14 March, 1825

Dear Sir:

Having understood that you are engaged in preparing to publish a history of this state and Mr. Hannahan having suggested that you would gladly receive any information on any subject relative to such a work; I have thought it might not be unacceptable (Nay that it would be serviceable) if I should offer you a few hints to aid you in the compilation of its Literary History. Should they be deemed of any use, you can avail yourself of them and I shall be gratified in that event.

In the year 1794 I opened an Academy in Columbia County, where a number of men who have since distinguished themselves received their Classical and Scientific Education, who never graduated nor attended any college, viz. W. H. Crawford, Thomas W. Cobb and Eldred Simkins of South Carolina. I removed into South Carolina in 1801, where you knew me.

With the origin of Franklin College and its History, you are probably better acquainted than I am until my accession in 1819.

On the 21st May I arrived here and entered on my duties forthwith, having been appointed on the 1st March preceding. On my arrival I found the college nearly extinct, consisting of only seven students with three professors.

A commodious building for a preparatory school has been since erected, in which two Tutors have been employed for four years past to instruct generally from 50 pupils to 100 and fit them for entering College. These Tutors are employed by the Board of Trustees with a salary of $800 each per annum. There are now in the College Faculty a President, Professor of Mathematics and Astronomy, a Professor of Natural Philosophy and Botany, a Professor of Chemistry, Mineralogy and the French Language, Geography, Antiquities, etc. The present number of the students is 103. Board is $12 per month. Tuition in College is $36 per annum; and in the Preparatory School, it costs nothing, as the Tutors are paid out of the friends of the University.

During the past year there has been much improvement and generally great good order in the Institution. And I do not believe I hazard anything in saying that a truly useful education may be acquired here as at most Colleges in the United States. I am confident that the Officers are both competent and as faithful now in the discharge of their official duties as at any other.

Some young men of uncommon promise have graduated here within the last three years who are industriously ascending the hall of fame.

I forgot to mention John C. Calhoun who commenced his study with me in Columbia County-- prosecuted them in Abbeville and graduated at Yale in 1804.

There are two large brick buildings each 120 feet long and 45 wide, one three story containing 24 rooms and the other four stories with 32 rooms and fireplaces for accommodation of the students. Also, a brick building Chapel for the Commencement and collegiate exercises of Religion and two elegant Halls for the Demosthenean and the Phi Kappa Literary Society. These Societies, comprehending nearly all the students in College, are sources of great improvement, employing each Saturday forenoon in these halls in Literary exercises. A library of about 1200 volumes occupies a room in the new College.

If you have seen Dr. Ramsay's "History of South Carolina" till 1808, I would suggest the plan of it as a good one. He wrote to me before he published it that he had adopted Henry's History of England as the Model which pleased him best, viz. to place all events and historical facts of the same kind and relating to the same general subject under one head, as the "Military History," "the civil history," "the Literary History" and each continuously.

You will excuse this scrawl written in very unusual haste and make use of it as your prudence may dictate. With unaffected wishes for your success and happiness, I am sincerely

                Your friend,

                M. Waddel

After resigning in 1829, Waddel waited around several months to return to Willington. He may have stayed in Athens that long to tidy up his business affairs, but he may also have delayed the trip because of the precarious condition of his wife, who had cancer. On the day in 1830 when Waddel was finally ready to leave, as his carriage stood in readiness before his house, the students of the college marched in a body to his house. One of them delivered a farewell speech for the student body.

A description has been left of what the man getting into the carriage looked like. "A leading divine of the straitest of all sects, he had then (about 1829) much of its antique formality and air of being buckled up in rigour and precision--looking such as Cotten Mather must have looked.... In his customary canonicals of dress, manners and countenance, he seemed terribly the austere polemic and the fierce pedagogue...a sort of Aristarch of the South."[12] (Aristarch, a severe Greek critic who rejected many of Homer's lines as forgeries, was the prototype of the strict critic.) When the farewell speech was over, Dr. and Mrs. Waddel climbed into the carriage. After Ben, their black coachman, cracked the whip, the carriage rolled away, carrying the minister of Mather-like antique formality, as the crowd waved goodbye. As Dr. Waddel left the University of Georgia in the grand manner, the only possible defect occurred when "Aristarch," who chewed tobacco excessively, leaned out of the carriage window to spit as the coach rolled on, taking him back to South Carolina.

MINISTER

Waddel was a man of genuine compassion and utter sincerity. He had no unorthodox religious views to make people think, and he was rigidly respectable in his morality. Such qualities made him a good local pastor. One of Calvinism's chief defects in practice, its tendency to equate proof of election with prosperity and social respectability, is demonstrated by Waddel's sermon texts. He preached, "He that covereth his sins shall not prosper" (Proverbs 28:13) and "For thou, Lord, wilt bless the righteous" (Psalm 5:12),[1] and his ministry, unlike that of Jesus, was completely limited to the socially respectable.

In view of the fact that the ministry was not Waddel's main occupation, that his health was never good, and that the modes of travel were very primitive, his pastoral record among those whom he did serve is remarkable. One sign of his care and concern is that he kept a record of sermon texts and where he preached them from 1819 to 1836, because he used the same sermon frequently and wisely did not wish to repeat a sermon in the same church.

During his career he served on some sort of regular basis the churches at Johns Island, Dorchester, Hopewell, Willington, Liberty and Rocky River in South Carolina and Mount Carmel and Athens in Georgia. The record shows that he preached in at least eighty different churches in South Carolina and Georgia, many of them more than once, as well as performing his regular duties. This total does not count prayer meetings, funerals, baptisms, camp meetings, college chapels, and addresses at Bible Societies. He preached as a guest in prominent Presbyterian churches in Georgia such as Independent Church, Savannah; First Church, Macon; First Church, Augusta. In South Carolina he preached at First Church, Columbia, and at Scots Kirk and Circular (Congregational) in Charleston.

He preached by invitation to the Governor and legislators of Georgia in the State House at Milledgeville and in Columbia to the legislature of South Carolina.[3] When he held Holy Communion in Pendleton, South Carolina, John C. Calhoun and his wife attended.[4] Governor McDuffie when at his nearby plantation home, "Cherry Hill," attended Waddel's services regularly.[5] In Columbia Waddel stayed at the home of Colonel Thomas Taylor, upon whose plantation the city of Columbia was founded,[6] a pious and wealthy Presbyterian planter.

The sincerity of Waddel's conversion to the ministry is seen in that the local adulation did not affect his sense of mission at all. He still headed out to carry

the Gospel to the congregation at Goshen, Georgia, went
to Rehoboth Church near Hard Labor Creek in South Carolina
to preach to "eleven souls," crossed rivers in canoes to
get to preaching, and even filled the pulpit at the Trail
Creek Baptist, a foot-washing congregation with very
informal worship, whenever he was asked, which was often.

While Waddel contributed to social organization, he
never stopped doing good to individuals: "Preached...at
William Spear's Esquire, for his aged step-mother." He
hastened to the bedside of the dying" "Was awakened
out of a sound sleep about thirty minutes past 2:00 a.m.
to go to see Mr. Harris--stayed with him till he died
about one half past three." He finished a month in his
diary with the prayer, "May God guide me and influence
me to love him more and serve him better." With all his
faithfulness, however, Waddel never worked the magic
in his churches that he did in his schools. If he had
been able to spank his parishioners as he did his students,
he might have worked wonders.

Furthermore, though much in demand, he was not a
particularly good preacher. His sermons were too long
and his language blunt. Certain points recurred regularly[7] so that anyone who had heard a few of his sermons
had heard them all. He was no rhetorician but he at
least did not read his sermons. He divided his sermons
into the usual three parts and took, sometimes extempore,
each of the three major sections in depth, using "once
more" and "again" over and over. At the conclusion of
each division he used the word "finally," which usually
perked up his congregation--until they learned Waddel
was not at his sermon's end until the third "finally."
Some listeners, predictably, found this tedious. Boys
at the University of Georgia, irritated over his constant
use of "finally" and his interminable sermons, ventilated
their feelings. Over the chapel pulpit where he preached,
they wrote in large letters, "I do not wish to be tedious;
once more, finally, and again!"[8] Naturally such criticism
had no effect on Waddel's sermons. In typically Scotch-
Irish fashion he was as averse to change as the Presbyterian elder who is supposed to have prayed, "Lord, let
me be right, since I am uncommonly hard to turn around
when wrong."[9]

There is a touching picture of Waddel as an old,
venerated, and famous man suffering from "rheumatics"
bravely preaching to "a few in the forest." Waddel,
who uncharacteristically had a sense of humor about all
this, wrote, "I preached 'sub dio' in the open air."
He was proud of his triumphs; when a crowd attended
preaching, he said, "Many attended although the Methodists
had a camp meeting in the vicinity." He noted the
tribulations of his hearers: "Conversed with Chambers
who was in great soul distress"; and the delights of a

camp meeting: "Much excitement after night. Some professed conversion." He attacked his listeners' practices in his preaching: "Spoke of cards..spoke of female profane swearing." In his diary he even justified his actions to himself: "Preached Major Hill's funeral. Although he was a Baptist, yet he was very liberal in sentiment."

The area in which Waddel's influence was forward-looking and actually served rather than hindered the Presbyterian Church was in being an ordinary active presbyter, or elder, participating in advancing the organizational life of the church. Waddel, along with four other teaching elders (pastors) and four ruling elders, set up the Presbytery of Hopewell, the first in Georgia. The first meeting of the Presbytery, a church governing court consisting of ministers and representative elders within a district, was on March 16, 1797, at Liberty Church near Washington. The initial statement of Georgia's first Presbytery sounded very much like Waddel: "The Presbytery having taken into view the degeneracy of manners and the declension of Religion which so awfully prevail;...do earnestly recommend that the first Tuesday in January, April, July and October be hereafter observed as days of humiliation, fasting and prayer."[10]

When Waddel went to the *University of Georgia (Franklin College) in 1819 to be its president, he found that Athens had no Presbyterian Church. Along with fourteen others he founded the First Presbyterian Church of Athens in 1820. The church was too small to be able to afford a resident minister, so Waddel served until he left Athens in 1829 as the church's stated supply, an official term for a minister who is not permanent but serves. The congregation met in Apparatus Hall, then in the college chapel, until in 1828 a sanctuary was built with a high red pulpit from which Waddel preached. While in Athens, Waddel was active in organizing an Education Society, made up largely of Presbyterians, which assisted worthy young men in furthering their schooling for the ministry--an early scholarship service. Alexander Stephens, Vice President of the Confederacy, was one poor boy enabled to go to college on this money.

While Waddel was President, a good friend, Dr. Thomas Goulding, pastor at Lexington, Georgia, was training a few theological students at the manse. The Synod of South Carolina of which Georgia was a part, organized these into a seminary located at Columbia. Dr. Waddel was offered the senior professorship at Columbia Seminary soon after it was organized. His diary records that he reached Columbia on June 1, 1830, to preach the next night in the Presbyterian Lecture Room from Job 14:6. He was unwell on the trip back to Willington. At the Synod meetings of December 1830, according to his diary, he resigned his post: "resigned my appointment last night as Senior professor in Theological Seminary." The long, frequent trips were too much.

The attention paid to Waddel's preaching in his old age was largely due to the respect people had for him as a famous schoolmaster.[11] Unfortunately their respect diminished when the Reverend Dr. Waddel expected his congregations to toe the strictest Presbyterian line. For example, he did not travel on Sunday except to and from church; if he found himself in a town on Sunday, he observed the Sabbath there, then traveled again on Monday. When his church members did not observe all Calvinistic prohibitions, he spoke to them about their "sins." Some of his members did not appreciate his meddling morality.[12] Although in his school Waddel tried innovative techniques, in his churches his only new techniques were revival preaching and revival hymns, and of course even revivalism was no longer new in time.

The fact that Waddel was for revivalism made him somewhat objectionable to the conservative Old Light Presbyterians who did not believe that being "born again" in a crisis emotional experience was necessary for salvation. The Old Lights not only held that a person might develop in grace slowly instead of dramatically all at once but even believed that a person might be saved simply by being a member of the church covenant. In fact, there were enough areas of possible disagreement about Waddel to keep him from becoming the doddering fool of a pastor whom everyone loves. He was fortunate in that. But he did not have enough self-awareness to keep himself from being the famous old fool whose sermons stretched on and on. Although the Rocky River Church members, straining even Southern courtesy, put up with the one hour and forty-five minute ramblings that his sermons eventually became, it was because of his academic reputation.

Waddel's heart was always more in the pulpit than in the classroom. Yet as a teacher he was great, while as a preacher he was mediocre at best. This is the supreme irony of his career: what he wanted to excel in, he couldn't; what he was not as interested in, he did brilliantly. The sophisticate, looking at such frustrating facts, may simply say, "C'est la vie." Only Waddel was an overserious Calvinist who could not resign himself to the facts. A Christian who believed in every miracle of the Apostles' Creed was not one to let a few facts stand in the way. It was whatever seized Waddel's imagination that counted, and preaching seized his imagination more than teaching. It was enough to drive a preacher to a sermon on Ecclesiastes

6:12: "For who knoweth what is good for man in this life...for who can tell a man what shall be after him under the sun?"

REVIVALISM AND THE COLLAPSE OF THE COVENANT

In every age it is fashionable for clergymen to deplore the godlessness of the times. In his diary on February 5, 1834, Waddel records how he discussed the "declining state of religion." On February 14 he records that he "spoke of the state of the churches" to Squire Houston. As far as the Southern Presbyterians went, Waddel was right. The Calvinist ideal was supposed to be Genevan strictness, and the Scotch-Irish in Ireland had indeed had a very strictly disciplined church life. Even the Scotch-Irish emigrants in the back-country South among whom Waddel was reared kept a rigid Genevan discipline. However, as the Scotch-Irish became full-fledged Southerners, the bonds began to weaken.

The sensual and sunny South, after all, was not an ideal geographical setting for Calvinism, which would be most likely to thrive in a cold climate amid stinging winds, in a place where hard work is necessary to survive, a place characterized by the wearing of heavy clothes and by a bracing autumnal tang in the air. The Southern heat, by contrast, was not conducive to very hard work. Its flower-perfumed evenings were uncalvinistically tempting. Perspiration made heavy clothing a curse. Moral fibre weakened to a degree, but not enough to prevent the Scotch-Irish from being successful economically. Indeed, their work and thrift provided the capital for some of them to become plantation owners and merchants. Furthermore the Scotch-Irish emphasis on education encouraged and enabled them to rise to high places in the professions. The Scotch-Irish as a group were socially on the rise during the lifetime of Waddel.

As wealth grew, leisure increased, conspicuous consumption became possible, and rigid morality inevitably declined. The successful Scotch-Irish remained faithful to their denomination, but they began to raise the tone of Southern Presbyterianism to a more sophisticated level. This movement continued through the life of Moses Waddel, whose rigid Calvinism was in many ways buried with him. Waddel railed to the end on the decline and fall of the old morality.

An illustration of the decline of Calvinistic morals may be found in the experience of Theodore Clapp, an early Yale graduate. Clapp, a New England Congregationalist, came South in 1833 to serve the Presbyterians of New Orleans. He found the officers of the church "fine looking gentlemen with polished manners, well informed, so cheerful, easy, natural and agreeable" that he decided they could not be Presbyterians. He found, to his surprise, "the ladies and gentlemen in New Orleans dressed as finely to go to church as they did when they went to the opera, evening party or ball room."[1] He was even more shocked when he asked that the debt on the church building be paid and the congregation responded by having a legalized lottery to raise money. Nor can this gambling be blamed on the uniquely exotic atmosphere of New Orleans. The First Presbyterian Church of Columbia, South Carolina, raised its money by a lottery in 1814. The morally downhill tenor of things in Columbia can further be seen in that in 1813 when the Anglicans and Presbyterians, who had been sharing the same building, decided to go separate paths, the representatives of the congregations "rolled the bones"[2] to decide who would get the original site. This was in First Church, where John Taylor, Governor of South Carolina 1826-28, was later an elder. The Presbyterians, who won the toss and kept the lot, said that this method of decision was all right since in the Bible the casting of "lots" is mentioned.

Thoreau criticized the Puritans of New England for lack of spirited enjoyment, reminding them that the Westminster Cathechism states that the chief end of man was "to glorify God and enjoy him forever." The New England Puritans, Thoreau said, glorified but never seemed to enjoy. He was never aware of the Presbyterians in the South breaking out of the Calvinist mold and building a tradition of enjoyment, at least in some of the churches.

Conservative Southern ministers like Waddel, however, did attempt to enforce church discipline in the old ways. Ante-bellum church records are full of these doomed attempts. As early as 1809 at Scots Kirk, Charleston, an attempt by the Rev. George Buchan to establish another congregation with strict Calvinistic discipline failed so totally that Buchan departed the South in a nervous collapse.[3] In Wetumpka, Alabama, the elders and ministers of one congregation tried similarly--and just as fruitlessly--to oversee the personal habits of members engaged in horse racing, drinking, gambling, dancing, and other "fashionable amusements."[4] The elders of a church in Indiantown, South Carolina, in 1832-33 were so busy deploring these same practices of its members that when they erected a new sanctuary, they forgot to mention the fact in the church "minutes,"[5] which were filled with details about the "sins" of the membership. In 1857 a religious article in a Presbyterian magazine noted (seventeen years after Waddel's death) that church members were engaging in all sorts of "worldly amusements" with the "firm" belief that such practices were innocent.[6]

But Waddel and others like him fought bitterly all the way. To the end Waddel would make a special visit to any members of his congregation rumored to be dancing and would have a prayer meeting with them. The effectiveness of this may be gauged by Mary Moragne, a very pious young member of his church, who commented in her diary in 1836 that at a party of young Presbyterians there was dancing--"in spite of the bull the Presbytery issued."[7] (She danced herself.) Through the years Waddel became himself a "tough head," a derogatory slang term he had used when young to describe the conservative church elders opposing change. Any religious assessment of Waddel must take into account that he was a reactionary force in the healthy and progressive movement of Presbyterian morality in the South away from the legalism and literalism of Geneva.

The curse placed on Calvinism was its too literal attempt to bring the Kingdom of God to earth by descending to laws that forbade kissing on Sunday, laws against cooking on Sunday, laws that placed people in the stocks for a variety of Puritan offenses, laws against dancing, blue laws against many forms of human enjoyment, church laws interfering with liberty of conscience. Waddel fought steadily against any move away from the excessively particular literalism of Geneva to a greater freedom of individual conscience and the liberty of the Christian man. To him and other tough heads such a move was simply "the declining state of religion."

It is against this backdrop of what Waddel saw as a degenerating Presbyterian faith and his fear that the spiritual chaos of the Low Country would spread elsewhere that his devotion to revivalism must be understood. This devotion explained his interest in reading Jonathan Edwards. As a Presbyterian minister Waddel had naturally been trained on the books of Dr. Edwards, briefly President of Princeton the social and intellectual center of Scotch-Irish Presbyterianism. The fact that Dr. Edwards was America's most intelligent revivalist made his books popular at Hampden-Sydney in its 18th century period of revival. Waddel's diary shows that he had a genuine interest in Edwards. On one occasion for four straight days (November 8-11, 1824) Waddel's diary contains the notation that he "read Edwards."

The problem of Jonathan Edwards in New England was similar to that of Waddel in the South and must be understood sociologically. Edwards faced in New England the secularization of society and what seemed to him the degeneration of the old New England Congregational Calvinist covenant. Revivalism became his method of trying for widespread conversions so that the covenant might be restored and the increasing secularization of New England society arrested. Although such a task was impossible since time could not be turned back to Geneva or old New England, Edwards still manfully tried to reclaim New England for the covenant. Thus he preached his famous revivalistic masterpieces to arouse interest in religion. He was held responsible for beginning a spiritual "awakening" or revival. Waddel by training and inclination felt an Edwards frustration, bordering perhaps on paranoia, over this secularization. Religiously his was a move to restore the Scotch-Irish Presbyterian covenant in the South by revivalism. It too was doomed by the forces of secular history as effectively as its New England precursor.

Waddel had been trained at Hampden-Sydney to forego the more obvious emotional excesses of the free sects, the Methodists and Baptists. Furthermore, sincerely believing as he did in the necessity of an educated clergy, he was in his preaching under some Presbyterian scholarly restraint. Aside from these qualifications, however, he was heart and soul a revivalist. As a "New Light" or "New School" Presbyterian, Waddel was a believer in emotionalism and revivalism. One of his students, John Walker, wrote to Dr. Waddel in 1803 that Waddel's preaching was quite different from that he found at Princeton, where Dr. Holleck, for instance, actually read his sermons--a practice which Walker felt destroyed the "vitality" and "fervor" of religion. Dr. Waddel exhibited more fervor when he delivered his sermons.

Waddel rarely missed an opportunity for a revival, camp meeting, or protracted meeting. He had yearly revivals at Willington, and on one occasion he gave special holidays to the University of Georgia students to attend a Methodist camp meeting. At the school at Willington, made up of teenagers and impressionable young people, a contemporary relates that some students came near losing "their physical and mental health" due to prolonged and high-pitched religious emotionalism. Indeed, "came near" was a euphemism; the witness himself became almost psychologically blind. Some adolescents cracked mentally, never to fully recover. One student became "painfully and morbidly sensitive in his conscience." Another became "utterly absorbed" in his devotional life and for the rest of his life appeared absent-minded and moved his lips constantly in "secret (though inaudible) prayer." The witness notes that "these persons were consistently Christian all their lives, not withstanding these peculiarities"[8] and that in 1812 half of the students at Willington were under deep conviction of sin while twenty were converted.

Deep conviction of sin, no small trauma, might best be described by Jonathan Edwards' thoughts on man in "The Justice of God in the Damnation of Sinners:" "A little wretched, despicable creature; a worm, a mere nothing, and less than nothing; a vile insect that has risen up in contempt against the majesty of heaven and earth."

Waddel's diary gives us a picture of a typical revival. On July 25, 1828, he "went early and alone (after buying a barrell of flour of Sloan at Mrs. Franklin's) to camp meeting in Jackson--arrived at 1:30 p.m.--preached at 3:00 p.m. on 2nd Timothy 3:7 ('Ever learning and never able to come to the knowledge of truth')." On Saturday, July 26, 1829, he "exhorted in Captain Cunningham's tent--preached at 11:00 a.m. from James 1:8--heard Mr. Wilson (another preacher) at 3:00 p.m.--conversed with several anxious people in my tent." (The "anxious people" in his tent were frightened that they were hellbound.) Here is the entry for Sunday, July 27: "Sabbath--spoke to many in tent--...preached to 1000 from Jeremiah 6:16 ('ask for the old paths...the good way, and walk therein, and ye shall find rest for your souls') and at night from James 1:8 ('A double-minded man is unstable')."

A description is left of the revivals of Rev. Robert Cunningham, one of five ministers who with Waddel formed Hopewell Presbytery. An Alabama woman who came to be revived became so excited by his Communion sermon that "after shouting some moments" she dropped dead.[9] On another occasion Cunningham, while exhorting a camp meeting, fell "on the ground insensible." When he came to, he said that he felt he had died and gone to heaven. He said that he looked down at his old dead body and regretted, that like an old coat, he would have to put it on again. He said that when he had to come alive again, he was miserable. The crowd admired this monologue greatly. This ecclesiastical performer apparently picked up the idea for his act from the Rev. William Tennent, the younger, who parlayed an apparent epileptic seizure into a perennially crowd-pleasing view of the afterlife. A man who attended a Presbyterian camp meeting in 1804 at a church of which Waddel would become pastor the next year recorded, "There was no noise, yet many would fall down and appear for hours insensible. But so far as my knowledge extends I could perceive no reformation in after life."[10]

As far as the Presbyterian denomination was concerned, revivalism as a method did definite harm. The Methodist and Baptist denominations gained greatly by emotional revivals, obtaining many of the ignorant Scotch-Irish that Presbyterians could not hold on the frontier. The ironic result of revivalism such as Waddel's was that Presbyterianism ceased to be a church of the people and became instead a "class" church, serving predominantly the educated and professional classes unswayed by revivalism and its primarily emotional appeals. The reason why the educated folk rejected revivalism is perhaps evident from a description of Mrs. John King of Athens who "spoke at camp meetings and love feasts and generally wound up the meetings."[11] Weighing at least 250 pounds, she ate fifty peaches at a sitting. Her religious testimony was that when Jesus appeared to her in her garden as he had done to Mary on resurrection day, she threw herself at his feet--surely an earth-shaking act. Even though Jesus, no doubt wisely, vanished, the sight of him left her with "peace and joy."

There was yet another bad effect of revivalism on the Presbyterians. Many of the hymns used in these services and revivals came from Isaac Watts' hymns. Waddel was one of many revivalists who advocated and brought about the use in Presbyterian services of these popular hymns, which in time came to replace the older Psalms. Advocating this change showed Waddel again to be religiously a man of zeal but considerable insensitivity, little foresight, and no grasp of aesthetic principles. In an ecclesiastical demonstration of Gresham's law the hymns which replaced the Psalms were very often unbelievably bad. The distinctive heritage of Psalm singing was soon lost. The cheap, vulgar, and sentimental hymnology which became the rule of worship probably reached its nadir when the Southern Presbyterian Hymnal of 1901 included an 1860 effort of Mrs. Elizabeth Codner: "Lord, I hear of showers of blessing, Thou art scattering full and free,...Let some droppings fall on me."[12]

THE DIVINE VISITATION

It has already been noted that Waddel read a large amount of Jonathan Edwards' writings. Perhaps the most important for Waddel was one with a typically interminable eighteenth-century title, <u>Edwards on Revivals: Containing a Faithful Narrative of the Surprising Work of God in the Conversions of Many Hundred Souls in Northampton, Massachusetts, A.D. 1735. Also Thoughts on the Revival of Religion in New England, 1742, and the Way It Ought to be Acknowledged and Promoted.</u> One edition of this book had the recommendation of the President and professors of Princeton and a preface partly written by Isaac Watts in 1737.

It is more than pertinent that the <u>Faithful Narrative</u> contains the story of the conversion of <u>Abigail Hutchinson</u>, who "was first awakened in the winter season, on Monday, by something she heard her brother say."[1] He said, as brothers will, that another young woman had been recently converted and that this has "generally affected the young people." According to Edwards, this news "stirred up a spirit of envy" in Abigail because she considered the other girl "unworthy of being distinguished from others by such a mercy." Having been given Abigail's psychology, we may work out her "predestination." She resolved to beat the other girl in the game of conversion. Soon she was in such terror over having "sinned against God" that she worked herself into a nervous state and became genuinely ill. On Tuesday "she told her brother in the morning that she had seen Christ last night." After this she gave many testimonies and became indeed a genuine fountain of clichés and simple-minded platitudes. She not only said that it was "pleasant to think of lying in the dust all the days of her life, mourning for sin" but even expressed downsight "longings for death." She became so sick that it looked as if these longings were to be fulfilled. Yet "when her brother was reading in Job, concerning worms feeding on the dead body, she appeared with a pleasant smile."

Abigail, an unusually silly adolescent, finally received her just reward for undermining her health with all this emotionalism. But nobody deserved the death she died of. Her throat stopped up so she could swallow almost nothing and that "which she took in flew out her nostril, till she at last" could not swallow anything. "She died as a person that went to sleep, without any struggling, about noon, on Friday, June 27th, 1735."[2] This was the sort of religious symptomatology that was held up as ideal to Waddel and of which he "read much.' The reason the miserable story of Abigail is pertinent is that Waddel's only book, <u>The Memoirs of the Life of Miss Caroline Elizabeth Smelt</u>, published in 1819, was obviously written under this influence.

103

The difference was that whereas Edwards knew how to turn a phrase and put in convincing detail, Waddel, a far poorer writer, simply pontificated. Instead of narrative there is boring pulpit rhetoric; however, the book made him a name with the evangelicals of the time. Two editions of The Memoirs were printed in England and three in America.[3] Misses Hutchinson and Smelt, gargoyles on the Cathedral of American Gothic, were nonetheless living people who come down to us highly verified as to their unhappy earthly existence. One piece of independent verification is from Waddel's diary, July 30, 1825: "Today a dreadful disaster befell Mrs. Walker and Mrs. Smelt by their horses running away with their carriages."

Caroline Smelt was the daughter of an Augusta physician, Dennis Smelt, U.S. Representative from Georgia 1806-1811.[4] Smelt, an alumnus of William and Mary, settled and later married in Augusta, where Caroline was born December 20, 1800. Whereas Abigail's problem was her envy of another girl whose conversion was drawing the attention of other young people, Caroline's problem was her mother, a neurotic with a religious monomania which she had contracted from a pious Scotch-Irish mother. Mrs. Smelt early imbued the girl with her own religious point of view. By age two Caroline had been taught and knew from memory "a number of short instructive lessons."[6] Even this description of precocity may be an understatement. At age five she threw a tantrum and refused to go to so wicked a place as dancing school. She is then quoted as saying to her mother--at age five--"I do not regard any reproaches my conduct on this occasion may bring upon me, if you will forgive me, and not desire me to go again."[7] The whole scene reeks of the maternal lamp. The study continues as Caroline grasps the "plan of salvation" at age eight.

When Caroline was sixteen, the family pastor was in bad health and not able to minister fully to his congregation including Caroline. The mother naturally felt a need to fill this gap by "the use of such methods and admonitions as might appear most proper to counteract the influence of the world."[8] She nagged unceasingly, dramatized religious situations, and hounded the girl with questions about her spiritual state. However, Mrs. Smelt never really succeeded in producing a religious experience until Caroline "expressed a desire to see" a dying orphan, as she had "never seen any person die."[9] This experience fulfilled the mother's wishes as the orphan died of a fever in a particularly disturbing manner: "I never had such feeling in all my life--I viewed with horror the change in her...I saw her struggles--the sight was more than I could bear...a convulsion came on."[10] Caroline went home and spent the night in bed

with her mother. Terrified of dying and even more of
hell, Caroline had a religious awakening which Waddel
thought quite commendable.

Around two weeks later, on the 28th of August,
Caroline showed symptoms of the deadly plague going
around. That night "a most violent fever came on"
her. The physicians bled her the next day, but there
was no improvement. Mrs. Smelt, true to the end, "was
not now pleading for the life of her beloved daughter
but for the salvation of her soul." She brought cheer
to Caroline's bedside: "My dear Caroline, you are now
on the bed of affliction; I hope you do not neglect
to call upon the Lord."[11] Fevered and delirious, she
was faced with one question: had she been born again?
The mother and daughter began praying together for a
"manifestation." Between the emotionalism and the
delirium of the fever, the girl finally cracked. Later
when her physician-father was reaching for her wrist
to feel her pulse, she began singing hymns. She continued, completely unaware of anyone or anything around
her, for a half hour. "When her mind returned to the
consideration of objects around her," she told "what
the Lord had done for her soul--that He had baptized
her with the Holy Ghost."[12] When she started singing
again, it was "affirmed by all who were present, that
they never heard or read of anything more angelic."[13]
Before dying she quoted a rather lengthy piece of
scripture, worried about her cousin Cornelia's unen-
lightened soul, and commented, "it is sweet to die;
death is a pleasant friend--the gate of heaven."[14]

Waddel in a conclusion to the book moralizes, "We
may hence observe the inestimable advantage which may,
and often does, arise from early instruction in the
doctrines and duties of the Christian religion." But
of course his views on Christian education were a minor
part of the narrative. The important factor to Waddel
was that she "received satisfactory evidence of her
interest in Christ" on the "fifth day after her last
illness," that is, when she lay, Ophelia-like, singing
obliviously in the bed. Waddel believed this was an
example of a divine visitation. "Could anything short
of supernatural power," he rhetorically asks, "have
inspired a tender, timid and delicate young female
with such confidence...?...In no other way than by
ascribing her triumph over death...to Him."[15]

Waddel never knew Caroline but was relying on facts
brought to him after her death. As this black-clothed
servant of God heard the morbid story of Caroline,
drinking in every detail of death and conversion, he
seems to have felt a kind of spiritual intoxication
that may have made his pulses quicken. Here was divine
proof from God such as Dr. Jonathan Edwards had described.

Waddel's macabre Gothic mind momentarily experienced a sense of exaltation. He must record the Divine visitation, the proof of election, the sealing kiss of God on his bride, the Church.

The Memoirs of the Life of Miss Caroline Elizabeth Smelt (1819) cannot be dismissed as Professor Yates Snowden did by saying, "a miserable little goody-goody Sunday school book."[16] Seen in the context of Jonathan Edwards and the revivalistic movement, it has definite meaning. It verified the visiting of the Holy Spirit to the elect of the South, thereby legitimizing Southern Puritanism. It showed the South to be as blessed as the New England and Princeton of Edwards' day. It showed Georgia as a place where God's work was being carried on in the grand manner. It placed the seal of God on the type of born-again religion being carried by revivalists like Waddel all through the South to people who gathered to eat dinner on the grounds and to enjoy the spirits of their choice. It was a notification to the Puritan world by a native-born Southern Puritan that Georgia had arrived religiously. As a harbinger of Southern equality and Southern nationalism, The Memoirs was probably the first book written by a native Southern Puritan to record a special proof of God's blessing on Dixie.

In Waddel's eyes the book is a legitimization, a proof of the young woman's election. As he first drank in the details of this pitiful adolescent's life, he must have felt like a prophet discovering a special messenger from God. His duty to write this, his one and only book, was clear, and its acceptance in England among evangelicals was no doubt heart-warming. However, the book's undeniable meaning still does not make any less morbid this tale of an O'Connor-like Southern "freak" and her neurotic mother.

The book, in fact, simply makes obvious the fact that Waddel's religion was a decadent Calvinism spiked with hyper-emotional revivalism, cheap hymnological sentimentalities, New England neuroses, and divine hallucinations. Such religion followed as a reaction against the ebbing of the Calvinistic covenant in New England and among the Southern Scotch-Irish. Not being broad-minded enough or tolerant enough to see the decline of the Covenant as a healthy step away from a too restrictive legalism and literalism, ministers like Waddel turned to sermons on hellfire to scare their members and force them back to religion. This technique often worked, but whatever it was, it was not ever true Calvinism. These unhealthy-minded people that jerked, rolled, fell down dead, barked like dogs, starved themselves to death, and testified immoderately would have disgusted John Calvin as the biggest group of Anabaptists ever gathered to blaspheme God.

Waddel's mind was truly trained in the Calvinistic attitude of frustration over the secularism of the times. It was a religious position fast fading with the intelligent young. John C. Calhoun, who was genuinely fond of Waddel, looked at his semi-paranoid, reactionary Calvinism and rejected it. He went so far as to say later, "Unitarianism is the only true faith and will ultimately prevail over the world."[17] (Yet, even as Calhoun was pontificating, Ralph Waldo Emerson was asking, "Where are the second generation Unitarians?") The fact has to be faced: some aspects of Waddel's faith were repugnant. His morality was distorted on priorities and therefore unbalanced. His view of God was sometimes so macabre that it has repelled historians and caused him to receive little of the fame he deserves. But posterity can hardly be blamed for not inviting to the banquet of fame a morbid presence who looks upon all pleasures--dancing, drinking, card playing, betting, horse racing, Sunday sports, and novel reading--and croaks, "Nevermore."

Though Waddel, caught up in his ministry, was unaware of the fact, his best work was in education. It is an evaluation Waddel would not have accepted because he had a religious obsession, but it was a common one. Meigs, a biographer of Calhoun, summed Waddel up rightly when he said, "This gentleman, whose real function on earth was surely the teaching of boys, seems to have forever had a hankering after the pulpit."[18] And Meigs was right to specify "of boys." Any man who believed that young girls spoke, acted, or thought the way Caroline Smelt did in the Memoirs obviously knew little about them. It was fortunate that Waddel taught only boys at Willington.

THE CALVINIST PARADOX

Puritans were people with the right general aspirations and the wrong particular applications. When Waddel got away from Calvinistic legalism and excessive literalism in his preaching, the Gospel he preached was sane enough and even attractive. He saw the enjoyment of God as He expressed Himself in creation and salvation, as the principle behind Christianity. God was sovereign and loving. It was when the Puritans, such as Waddel, began their literal descent to practical applications that the sublime theory often degenerated into ridiculous stands on cards, dancing, and alcohol, and began delving into matters of personal taste and blue-law keeping. It was the Calvinist irony that the right aspirations as applied became ridiculous.

It was very difficult to keep the Puritan mind focused on God as shining and inspiring, and not concentrating on picky things which often brought disaster. It was a dilemma at the heart of Puritanism. And while not all Puritans were Calvinists, all too often Calvinists were puritan in temperament and outlook. But the great and elevated theories of John Calvin that began by elevating men to the stars, to an awareness of the sovereignity and divine love of God, tended to plummet down to explode into a shower of blue laws, legalisms, literalisms, personal meddling, a generally negative attitude to life, and finally refined prissiness that made a grim cell out of merry earth. Waddel was very much the tool of this Calvinistic backlash.

It was unfortunate but true that there were any number of trivial subjects on which Waddel delighted to rave. He regarded profanity as a sin of the worst kind; he could preach for a full hour on card-playing, and he even became a temperance advocate. However, it was not enough that he abide by these prohibitions; others had to do so, too. One can readily sympathize with the student at the University of Georgia, subjected to one of his lectures, who used as his excuse for being late to class that he had just been bored by the President for an hour and one half.[1]

It was non-transcending faith: pure intentions of a good-hearted man in practical application made him a bore. Non-transcendentally used the logic of Calvinism but lacked a certain saving sanity, as perhaps any theory carried to a flat and final conclusion will become ridiculous. (Indeed Waddel's death can be traced to a stroke that resulted from an attempt to carry logic too far.) Perhaps it is simply that those who try to take the Gospels literally always seem unbalanced in everyday life, or even more simply that overwhelming earnestness easily becomes tragicomic in the end. Whatever the difficulty may be, Waddel was the victim of it. If Christianity were a piano, he played with his elbows.

The picture that emerges from Waddel's searching the horizon with a spyglass to see who was going to a drinking house on the University of Georgia campus is essentially ludicrous, with overtones of low comedy. Waddel was not a fool, only an excessively earnest man without saving sanity to let him know when morality stopped and humor started. He never saw anything wrong with his meddlesome ways. That the master of Willington who gave students a right to jury trial by peers could not see that a spyglass was an infringement on the right of privacy is just one more of the Puritan paradoxes that made him what he was. The irony was that Calvinism was supposed to be logical and therefore consistent, but some applications were ludicrous against the light of lofty aims. The fact is religious law used without that divine transcendence which gives flexibility boomerangs or backlashes into ludicrousness. This is, perhaps, not fair but it is fact. It is what the great preacher in Ecclesiastes had seen when he cautioned, "be not righteous overmuch."

Waddel believed he was elected by God or predestined to salvation before the beginning of the world, but paradoxically he was constantly taking part in revivals that assumed free will and preaching in churches that assumed free will as axiomatically as his own denomination denied it. His revivalism at Willington that sometimes caused nervous breakdowns in boys was a yearly catastrophe. Although his diary records that he drank wine for his health, Waddel organized a Temperance Society and in 1830 was president of the Willington Temperance Society.[2] Waddel as a puritan felt called upon to mind everyone else's business in certain matters. It was again the paradox of Calvinism that the sublime theory of virtues ended in removing wine from the chalice at the Lord's Table, although the Disciples had drunk it. The sublime had become ridiculous in application. Strangest of all, it never seemed to occur to Waddel in 1819 that his ability to go out on a full-time evangelism circuit was paid for by the work of slaves. However, this paradox may be logically attributed to the normal tendency of everyone, including Presbyterians of the South, to accept the customs of their society as normal. St. Paul, after all, did not hesitate to send a runaway slave back to his master.

Waddel was possibly normal in that he had no sense of priorities in his burning desire to concern himself with society's life. He accepted slavery but worried about novel-reading and profanity. He

talked about a Utopian Christian state but his idea
of one was hell. His teaching, his strong point,
was likewise shortsighted in its goals. He worked
to produce leaders, but he produced mostly three kinds:
teachers, ministers, and politicians. He had no
concept of the South's need for technical, trade,
or manufacturing leadership.

And in fact even the political leaders that
Waddel trained, although personally good men, had no
concept of social reform without the boundary of
accepted customs. Had Waddel taught them ideas of
social reform in some other guise than regular church
going and no cursing, the South might have profited
greatly. As Benjamin F. Peery, the South Carolina
Unionist, commented in 1853:

> What might not South Carolina now be
> if her Calhouns, Haynes, McDuffies, Hamil-
> tons and Prestons had devoted their great
> talents and energies to the commercial
> and internal improvement of the state,
> instead of frittering them away in political
> squabbles, which ended in nothing?[3]

Although every human being is a compilation of
inconsistencies, paradoxes, short-sightedness and
unbalanced priorities, these defects are not usually
claimed to be consequences of divine inspiration.
Many of Waddel's defects, however, could be directly
traced to some originally noble theory he held in the
name of religion. Worst of all, since he held them
in the name of religion, there was little reasoning
with him. He was himself living proof of the Calvinist
paradox: the noble motivations of a well-meaning
minister, when put into practical applications, had
resulted in a temperance bigot.

The sincerity of Waddel's religious sigh was
deep but morally non-transcendent. He had no deep
understanding of his religious circumstances or any
real grasp of the psychological motives behind his
own religious views. But he enjoyed religion immensely
because, by making him elected and important to God,
it added drama to his otherwise dull life. Ignorance
without drama is insupportable. But religious drama
where religion is presented as narrow, judgemental,
ultra-respectable, conventional, dry, chanceless,
and boring is really satire--as if the "drama" had
been written by the devil himself.

PLANTATION LIFE

Since Waddel refused a salary for preaching, everywhere he lived he was forced to farm as well as teach. Eventually he became a sizeable plantation owner, with an eleven-hundred-acre tract near Willington, four hundred acres of which were cleared for farming. Dr. Waddel's manse on the great road to Augusta, described as "new, elegant, and beautifully situated,"[1] had six rooms with all the accompanying farm outbuildings (slave quarters, separate kitchen, carriage house, barn, smokehouse and outhouse), with an additional small house nearby that served as his study.

With approximately twenty-three slaves on the plantation, he was by contemporary standards a small planter. Although he bought a few slaves (he noted on March 12, 1839, "visited old Mrs. Newton about buying her man, Dick"), most of the slaves were a dowry for Elizabeth Pleasants when she married Moses Waddel. It was the custom of the times for a Southern lady to bring slaves as a dowry. At least one New York girl who married a Southerner was disliked by her mother-in-law because she had not brought her son any "niggers."[2]

When Eliza Pleasants Waddel came home to the plantation from Athens in 1830, she came to die. She had developed cancer while living in Athens and had been operated on, without anesthesia, as was always true then, but the cancer continued to ravage Eliza Waddel and cause her intense pain. A decanter of laudanum, an opium preparation, was kept on the sideboard in the Waddel house for her, but it did not help much.

At the end of March 1830 the children not at home were sent for. On April 4, a Sunday morning, John Newton, a son who taught and lived at home, was awakened early and told his mother was worse than usual. She was subject to violent seizures of pain. When John went into her bedroom, she was walking about the room, leaning on Moses' arm. If she lay down the agony was unutterable, but while she walked she was in less if constant pain. As she walked she spoke little, and then only to pray shortly for relief.[3] She kept walking about until she collapsed and had to be returned to bed, but since the pain when she lay down was unbearable, only with difficulty could she be kept in the bed by two of her children. She kept trying to get up, although she did not have the strength to walk or even stand; and when she lay back the pain was worse. After eight hours of excruciating pain she finally sank back on the bed in the arms of a son and mercifully died.⁴ The family's nerves broke and they wept.

Elizabeth Pleasants Waddel was buried in the "grand and beautiful old oak grove" that was the Willington Presbyterian Churchyard. Eliza Waddel's obituary said her parting was "alleviated" by the knowledge she would see all of her children in heaven except for one who was not a church member. (John Newton was not a church member at this time.) It ended on this note: "May her friends each be enabled to say, 'let me die the death of righteous, and let my last end be like hers.'"⁵ Despite the euphoria of the obituary, however, one cannot help feeling sorry for Eliza Waddel and wondering what she got out of life. Then when one reads in Howe's History of the Presbyterian Church in South Carolina that she "was rewarded by the privilege of ministering for more than thirty years to the comfort of an eminent servant of Christ," it should also be added she had children, a nice house, several house slaves as servants and a position of prestige in the community.

After her death most of the family dispersed to various places in Georgia, only John staying at home to help. Moses was left more alone than he had been in years, although a white housekeeper was hired to look after him. He spent his time in preaching at the Willington and Rocky River churches and in looking after the plantation, where he grew cotton (twenty bales was the maximum), wheat, oats, and corn with the help of a hired overseer, Mr. Wells. Waddel was up-to-date enough to have a mule-powered gin and a press that compressed picked cotton into bales. For a fee of a dollar a bale he sent his crops by boat in Augusta, where the price of cotton was around fifteen cents a pound.⁶

In winter Waddel utilized the otherwise lost time of the slaves by having them make and repair the farm fences and clear new land. His women slaves had such tasks as picking peaches and apples, then slicing the fruits into pieces that could be dried in the sun.⁷ Waddel's diary on September 17, 1833, shows he went out into the fields where the slaves were picking cotton and encouraged the blacks with promises of hats. He felt his efforts at motivation were quite successful.

Moses' son, John, said that his father was so humane toward his slaves that in one large planter's opinion Dr. Waddel's treatment of them was going "to ruin all the Negroes in the neighborhood." John added that his father was so humane he "was not what was known as a very successful planter" but was able to make his family "comfortable without superfluous luxury" anyway.[8] John's impression is inaccurate on two counts. To begin with, Waddel made money as a planter since his expenses were limited to shoes, blankets and cloth to make the simple slave clothes. Waddel undoubtedly lived without ostentation but only because he had once been poor and was frugal Scotch-Irish to boot. More important, if Moses Waddel's treatment accorded to slaves was excessively humane, the treatment by other owners must have been a scandal. Waddel made his blacks work hard (with no real relief even in the winter), drilled them in the Bible and Westminster Catechism for sweet relief, dressed them down for idleness, and did not hesitate to beat them-- this one for laziness, that one for cursing before him. All in all, he was a strict master of his slaves.

However, slaves found ways to express themselves nonverbally. On July 8, 1834, when the blacks were clearing land--a hard job involving cutting trees and pulling up stumps and roots--one slave refused to work any more. When ordered back to work by the overseer, he still refused. When the other slaves refused to help the overseer subjugate him, the slave ran away and was able to stay away twelve days before he was finally brought back and whipped. More subtle ways of protest were also used. Since sugar was a valuable commodity in the Old South, it was restricted in use and kept locked away in chests resembling small blanket chests in the house, usually in the dining room. One day Waddel found that sugar was missing. After the blacks went to work, he searched the slave cabins but found none.

Waddel must have been considered a just man, however, because at the University of Georgia on September 20, 1824, his diary records that some students hurried to get him to prevent a slave from being abused nearby. Undeniably Waddel was capable of conscience pangs about the system of slavery. He wrote on January 26, 1831, that he "saw a drove of Negroes--14 chained--a most unpleasant sight." The reason why a Christian like Waddel accepted slavery was probably that slavery was accepted in the Divine Guide Book which the Calvinists used for the resolution of every possible type of question. The classical Calvinist argument was, if something were in the Bible, it was acceptable, but if it were not in the Bible, it was not acceptable. Indeed, in recognizing that all people, black and white, were equal in the Kingdom of God, Waddel was a step ahead of most Southerners. At Holy Communion on August 30, 1829 he notes, "Preached Communion sermon from John 16:33 ("Be of good cheer; I have overcome the world") and served a table of blacks and two of whites."

Over the plight of blacks he struggled with his rather narrow-minded congregation. Since at this time many Southerners did not admit blacks had souls, they saw little reason to convert them to Christianity. In spite of physical infirmity he went to a church meeting on September 1, 1833 to discuss the matter. He later wrote, "Met the session of Willington Church--disturbed about Mr. Pinney's preaching on the subject of his mission to Africa." Mr. Pinney, a student at Franklin College while Waddel was president, was a church missionary raising money for missions in Liberia. Due to the influence of Dr. Waddel, Mr. Pinney was able to preach to the church at Willington from II Corinthians 8:14 ("that now at this time your abundance may be a supply for their want...that there may be equality") and to take up a good collection of $23.00 for African missions. Tactfully Waddel had Pinney lodge with him instead of with a member on the congregation. Waddel gave him an additional $10.00 from himself next day along with $2.00 from a neighbor actually named John Bull. Considering that Waddel's congregation was living off cheap black labor, their cold reception of Pinney was predictable enough.

Waddel's belief that all men of every race had souls put him in advance of many in the South. Among the first to work for the religious education of slaves, he was made chairman in December 1833 of a special committee of the Presbytery on the religious instruction of slaves. Not until the 1850s did the religious education of slaves become widely accepted among the Presbyterians of the South when the Rev. Charles C. Jones of Georgia began a national drive among Presbyterians to publicize this cause.

When Waddel returned from Athens, he reopened the Academy at Willington, where he taught with his son, John Newton, from 1830 to 1833 and with another son, James Pleasants, from 1833 to 1836.[9] As usual, he kept boys as boarders at the manse. Fittingly these twilight years of Willington helped produce probably the most famous crusader for public schooling in the South, Jabez Lamar Monroe Curry. When Curry was in Harvard Law School in the 1840s, a speech made by Horace Mann on public schooling made a profound impression. Curry said that Mann's "earnest enthusiasm and democratic ideas fixed my young mind and heart." From that time forward Curry was a crusader for universal public schooling in the South in the spirit and power of Horace Mann.

Although a member of the Confederate Congress and a Confederate cavalry officer, Curry was able in his views to rise above ideas of putting down the black race and to become an advocate of equality of education for blacks and whites. In 1881 he was elected agent of the Peabody Fund, a charitable foundation to aid Southern education. As agent of the Peabody Fund Curry is credited with establishing state normal schools in twelve Southern states for both blacks and whites, and credited with impressing upon Southern legislatures their state responsibility for rural schooling. Through Curry's hands came "the main threads of educational progress in the South."

A liberal in his time, he proclaimed in a speech before a Jim Crow audience that it was "the proudest duty of the South" to school every child, black or white. When silence predictably greeted this announcement, Curry, a great orator, declared to the white audience, "I will make you applaud the statement." His oratory on educational equality became so eloquent and passionate that the assembly did applaud. Curry's influence helped to develop the Southern Educational Board that "practically transformed" educational conditions in the South.[10]

It was both ironic and fitting that the influence of Waddel, a slave-owner and private schoolmaster, would reach indirectly to the education of the black descendants of slaves as well as into universal public schooling in the South. Waddel's mentality never reached the heights of believing in educational equality but he was ahead of his day in admitting that black and white were equal in the Kingdom of God and in advocating religious instruction for slaves. Once these spiritual rights were granted, other practical rights sooner or later logically had to follow.

Clement Eaton, Southern historian, called Waddel a "typical cotton planter of the Piedmont"[11]; in other words, he had a smaller estate, a smaller house and fewer slaves than many low country planters. Still to be Moses Waddel--college graduate, author, doctor, retired college president, Presbyterian minister, master of Willington, owner of a plantation, slaves and a carriage-- all these made him rather a grand seigneur in his area.

In becoming part of both the landed gentry and the professional class, Waddel had come a long way from his birth in a log cabin in Iredell County. Yet Waddel never became a snob because he had always been one--not about family, as an aristocrat might be, but about the good society. By "good society" he meant people with values and schooling very much like his own, and by "undesireableness of society"[12] he meant people without his values. But behind these qualities there was a sturdy, backcountry frontier republicanism about him that prompted him on occasion to go to the fields and work, sometimes actually picking cotton in his fields alongside the Negroes. He did not hesitate to invite mule drivers to have breakfast with him.

On the other hand, Doctor Waddel unhesitatingly took part in some of the more polite aspects of an ante-bellum planter's life. He visited others, dined out, and was welcomed in big plantation houses and given the garden tour (he called it "receiving the house"). He talked on horseback about crops and religion or had his coachman drive him places: "Rode in my barouche to Squire Giles--spoke with him--went on Squire Hunter's and lodged comfortably," or found a piazza to sit on: "I sat an hour on the piazza and conversed with Mrs. Arnold." In these and other ways he took part in polite society. And as if seeking the politest possible society, he joined on May 2, 1836 an assemblage of other members of the gentry at the "Female school" to witness appreciatively the pageantry crowning Miss Collier "Queen of May."

DANGERS AND DEPTHS

Although Moses Waddel was never really well either mentally or physically, during his last years things became worse, partly because he was no longer as involved in work and activity as he had been in Athens. Furthermore, he felt lonely since Eliza had died and the children had scattered. As the years went by he did not feel as well even as he had once felt. He was still subject to severe and sometimes lasting bouts of depression. In September, 1833, in his diary he gave thanks "for some days of more calm and agreeable exercises of mind than usual." On November 25, 1834 he wrote, "My mind and my body were considerably disordered today." At such times preaching was still the best therapy he knew. When he was too ill to make it to the church, he dressed and preached to friends while sitting in a chair in the parlor of the manse. But beyond the depression were the frequent illnesses; again and again Waddel's cry in these years was the diary notation, "I am unwell." From 1824 to 1836 his diary shows he was unwell with often recurring complaints: sciatica, rheumatism, lumbago, vertigo, back pains, cholera, diarrhea, colds, hoarseness, heartburn, dizziness, being giddy, irregular pulse, a pain in his ribs, a pain of the shoulder, a pain in his bottom loin, and chronic constipation.

The treatment was of three kinds, all worthless. His physicians salivated him, that is, produced an unusual secretion of saliva, generally by use of mercury in the mouth, and thereby caused excessive spitting that flushed out his mouth. The physicians also bled him indiscriminately for rheumatism and other sicknesses. Even when Waddel's horse, Romulus, sickened, the poor animal had to be bled in the mouth. Laxatives or purges of various kinds were also suggested frequently: castor oil, pills, pepper tea with salts, and rhubarb. His laxative pills were reasonably strong. Waddel, who compulsively recorded such details, wrote on October 22, 1824, "took a pill, wrought twice." All three treatments were based, of course, on the purge theory that sickness was caused by excessive "humours" that had to be purged from the system to make recovery possible. Salivating, bleeding, and a profusion of laxatives were the methods used to make the necessary purges of the system.

On August 29, 1836, Moses Waddel, bothered with vertigo, got some pills from from a local physician. Then, trying with flat and literal logic to bring about a truly gargantuan flux that would resolve his health problem, he took twenty-one laxative pills. He wrote in his diary that the pills worked well in the night and next morning. On the next day, Tuesday, August 30, still feeling unwell, he took more laxative pills, which operated

equally promptly. Not surprisingly, he felt so bad he
quit tobacco chewing all day, and two days later on
September 1 he wrote he was "Diseased with a bowel complaint." His diary ends with that day. In the night of
September 5, 1836, he suffered a severe stroke that
paralyzed his right side and left him unable to speak
clearly. When his son Isaac went to see about him,
Isaac heard a "very unnatural sound" proceeding from the
doctor's bedroom, the sound of Dr. Waddel trying to
articulate but finding it impossible to do so.[1]

The Doctor lay helpless for three weeks, part of
this time in a coma. His case was said to be "a combination of paralysis and apoplexy." When Moses finally
came out of the coma and back into life, it was "very
readily seen" by his son "that the light of his once
clear intellect was now clouded, and that he was but a
shattered wreck of his former self."[2] His mind came
and went after that, and he was permanently paralyzed
on his right side. Unable to walk steadily because of
the paralysis, he bound that a cane was not sufficient
support as he dragged himself along, so he used a staff
"nearly as high as his head" as he walked.

After the first stroke Waddel gave up the church
at Willington in September, 1836 but remained as part-
time preacher at the church at Rocky River. As the
grey-headed old man went about his ecclesiastical duties
balanced by his staff held in a trembling hand, he seemed
very much the Old Testament prophet. After a second
and more severe stroke, which occurred on July 14, 1837,
a visitor came to call upon him and found him in bed:
"One arm lay heavily at his side. 'This right hand,'
Waddel said, raising it with his left, then letting it
fall listlessly, 'how much it has done! but it will
never do any more.'"[3] The next day when John C. Calhoun's
brother-in-law came to visit Waddel and brought with him
his nephew, John C. Calhoun, Jr., an onlooker commented
that Waddel was "animated by the sight of the son of a
pupil of which he is so justly proud." The brother-in-
law tried to make conversation upon the writings of the
Apostles, but Waddel could only point to his head and
say he was failing there.[4]

When he was partially restored, he called his children
in and suggested that they divide his estate between them.
Then Waddel gave up his last pulpit, preaching his farewell sermon at Rocky River on December 9, 1838. After
his estate was advertised for sale in the Charleston
Mercury on January 8, 1839,[5] he was in a last great
depression. A family friend said, "a hopeless and irrevocable gloom settled on his mind."[6] After he was taken
to live at Athens with his son, James Pleasants Waddel,
a classics professor at the University of Georgia,[7]
the sick old man made many trips back to Willington,

hoping to die there and to be buried beside his wife. Mary Moragne, the novelist, passing the Willington Church early on Sunday, September 15, 1839, saw Dr. Waddel sitting on the steps. She wrote in her diary, "Saw poor old Dr. Waddel sitting on the door steps of the church--he says that he has come back to die at Willington."[8]

He grew worse in July, 1840, seeming to lose control of his faculties and appearing not to be conscious. Dr. Church, an old friend who had succeeded him as president of the college, went to see him. Since Waddel appeared to be in a coma, several people in the room began to talk to each other of other things. When Dr. Church, entering the conversation, mentioned the name of a former Presbyterian clergyman, a voice, immediately recognized as Waddel's, filled the room, "I knew him well--one of the best men I ever knew." Then Waddel sank back into his stupor from which it was impossible to raise him.[9] Moses Waddel finally died very gently, slipping into sleep, on the morning of July 21, 1840, as the sun rose. In May, 1836, before the first stroke he had written in his diary as if he sensed something was coming to an end: "Have been graciously brought home through dangers and depths."[10]

When Mary Moragne heard the news of Dr. Waddel's death at church in Willington on Sunday, August 2, she went home and fancifully wrote to Dr. Waddel in her diary, "if spirits of the blest can look back upon this earth...regard thy beloved Willington, every stone of which can attest thy worth, thy sterling inflexible virtues."[11]

An agnostic might not attribute the resolution of Dr. Waddel's life to grace, but the fact of his social worth to the South as well as his having personally gone through "dangers and depths" in his own life cannot be contested. Dr. Waddel made worthy social contributions, particularly in teaching and academic administration. He had also emerged time and time again from the dangers and depressions of mental disease in his series of breakdowns and passed through the depths of tragedy in his the death of his first wife, Catherine Calhoun, and the later death of a son and his namesake, Moses, Jr., one of his children by Eliza. Waddel's religion enabled him to tap his inner resources. His preaching and praying dug in that crust of custom we call personality as an oil well does the earth's crust, pumping up vast amounts of potential energy from unseen depths. His use of this energy was well put and, more often than not, wise. It was in his eyes, as he had often chanted in the early American revival hymn, grace, "amazing" grace. It had finally led him home.

EVALUATION

Dr. Waddel set his sails and never veered. He did what he set out early in life to do. At the end few people can say that. He set out from Hampden-Sydney College in Virginia in 1791 to devote his life to Christian service to the community. He served both the denomination he drew religious sustenance from and the community he lived in. For him teaching was a form of non-denominational Christian service. By any standards, Waddel gave Christian service. The Doctor was a veritable tidal wave of Christian service that elevated, innundated, swamped and ran over, carrying all before it. He taught brilliantly, prepared boys academically, changed others' characters, founded academies that became famous, used innovative teaching techniques, saved a college that would become a prominent university, established churches, held revivals, served Holy Communion, preached in the forests and got there by foot and canoe, maintained black slaves had souls, supported missionaries, ran a plantation and did unnumerable personal good deeds as he supported innumerable charities. He was a pioneer in Southern education, one whose record has not been beaten yet, a father of the University of Georgia, a founding father of Presbyterianism in Georgia, and a prominent figure in evangelical religion. Yet this came from a man who was always genuinely sickly, buried, so to speak, in the woods by choice, and who had regular, if intermittent nervous breakdowns. If ever a preacher could say, faith is the victory, it was he.

But, as with all tidal waves, there was a backlash to follow the wave. He was often at cross purposes with himself because he never really realized at what he was best. His morality had all the appeal of a strait jacket. His ethical emphases were distorted. In earnestness he could be ludicrous. He was in the habit of meddling and calling it his duty. His mind could be painfully conventionally rigid. He had a hot temper. He was considered to preach forever in a day when people liked long sermons. He had a breakdown at every conceivable opportunity of what were then called "nerves." (He was probably an obsessive compulsive for what the label is worth.) He was the representative for an age going back after the excesses of the French Revolution rather than going forward. He advocated mass emotionalism in revivalism as the answer.

Intellectually Waddel's life and attitudes were a reaction against the excesses of the enlightenment. He was one small part of a vast reaction to it and a consequent re-formation around principles of human behavior that emphasized the irrational and suprarational. This reaction included rediscovery of creeds, orthodoxy, and intuitive or mystical thought--in brief, religious romanticism. This reaction was a natural result of a period a period of starvation of man's subconscious needs in the "Enlightenment." Waddel's brand of romanticism involved the belief that in prayer he could contact and be guided by God. Yet this was no more--or less--romantic than Emerson's belief that man could contact and be guided by the "oversoul." Waddel, who liked Emerson relied fundamentally on feelings, believed that by being in touch in some strange way with their inner selves, they were guided by genuine feelings that were probably more helpful than anything that a highly rationalized logical process could have afforded them.

How Waddel arrived at his educational methods and structures is interesting but not as important as the fact that he arrived at them--and arrived at them long before many others did. Possessed of a quite ordinary mind, he was yet able to build a striking and original conception at Willington, just as an engineer who may be perfectly conventional socially can go to the office and design a breathtaking work. Waddel was sober and even compulsively conventional as a personality, but he was able to plan and carry through an experimental new educational design.

What he did was to create a unique school, an innovative and experimental school that worked. Within reasonable limitations the students were happy, the subject matter was well-learned, democracy was taught, morals were changed, and leaders were produced. This is no small accomplishment at any time under any circumstances. Compared to Willington, even Waddel's far better-known success in saving the University of Georgia is secondary indeed.

But Waddel's accomplishment at Willington has been relatively neglected for all-too-obvious reasons. The Willington accomplishment occurred in the South, an area considered educationally backward, and in antebellum times, an era considered romantic but meaningless and irrelevant. However, although Willington was in the South, it had more in common with the Calvinistic schools of New England than with any traditional Southern stereotypes. Furthermore, there was an inevitable forward-looking atmosphere at Willington; it belonged more to pioneers than plantation owners, more to the frontier heritage than the slave-owning heritage. Waddel, in fact, looked down on the Anglican faith of Charleston and the Low Country, and indeed nearly everything about it. That he helped produce Calhoun, worshipped in Charleston as the defender of everything "Southern," is a delicious irony.

All the methods and teachers that make up successful education should be studied. There has not been so much of it that we can afford to overlook any of it. Human nature changes little enough that what worked yesterday may, with modifications, work better than a present method. And what worked yesterday for a man ahead of his time may work for far more people today. Our schools today are far behind what Waddel was doing at Willington nearly two hundred years ago. To begin with, Willington students picked their academic level and went from there as fast as they wanted to go. There were no required activities outside of classes, and the teacher called the class finished only when the work was done. Mastering the subject matter taught not only intellectual content, but the need for precision, careful analysis, patience, and concentration. There were disciplinary innovations as well. Students who behaved incorrectly were punished in a way that involved the judgement of their own peer group. Students learned self-reliance and right use of freedom by having to do things for themselves like gather wood (or else go cold in the winter). The teacher went to the boys' rooms, took a personal interest in his students, and tried to give good counsel. The students had a spacious area of farm and forest to roam about unsupervised except by monitors whose duty they understood. The result was not chaos but students who did more homework than those at any other school, who were motivated, who tried to please in class. The students thought very highly of the school, and although they were usually in some awe of Dr. Waddel as students, they were always fond of him later.

This might be compared with the average present experience, in which a student goes where he has been placed by the faculty who have tested everything but his possible motivation. He may then go in lockstep with thirty other students, inching his way through a text that has to last for three months. When the class begins, he knows he will be safe as soon as a bell rings, and when the term is over, he will probably be promoted even if semi-literate. Neither preciseness, analysis, concentration, or patience is required by the carefully digested text, which was carefully written by an expert to be read, seemingly, by morons.

If the bored, resentful adolescent becomes unruly and is hauled up before justice, what he receives may not be justice in his eyes but the will of a semi-dead adult--"them"--trying to stifle the still living--"us." As for counseling he must get it across the desk from yet another adult whom he may not know and whose opinion he may not respect and who is paid to counsel since the teacher obviously does not care. The teacher has the several classes of forty-five minutes a day and changes semesters every four months, so individual interest is almost impossible. The result is often students who are apathetic, who are not motivated, to whom the idea of voluntarily doing more homework is laughable, and who come to class to pass exams, not to learn. They may have very little self-reliance taught either at school or home.

Willington shows what the frontier was capable of. Few schools of today are up to Willington in techniques, structure, and methods, but with our present wealth and technology there should be no reason we cannot come closer to the successes of Willington. Waddel's academies, however, also show us what is not the way to success: seeking to solve American educational problems by throwing money at them. Willington suggests the best money spent is on the teacher who can teach, or on the administrator who can design social structures. The rest is a matter of far less importance. Poor teachers in expensive buildings with thousands of dollars of equipment remain poor teachers.

Willington was neither a traditional or progressive school as we today think of these terms. Willington balanced both demands successfully. Waddel was able to use innovative methods and a redesigned school structure to forcefully teach a traditional or classical discipline. The example of Willington would suggest that education today, in its polarization into traditional versus progressive schooling, is making a vast mistake.

The principal defect in Willington was possibly that Waddel, on a recommendation of a jury of students, spanked; and it may be that too much is made even of Waddel's spankings. Although perhaps any acceptable non-violent punishment can replace it, the very fact that Dr. Waddel found such treatment necessary for tough plowboys may suggest that it is applicable to similar carefully considered situations. Violence may not solve the problem of original sin, but it might purchase a truce of temporary submission in which something more positive can be worked out. It is not realistic to discount completely in advance the effectiveness of violence in any and all situations. History will not support such logic.

Willington, an extraordinary conception launched by Moses Waddel, was a brief and brilliant meteor which faded away after him but left a trail of stars. Moses Waddel was the South's first modern teacher and the greatest practical genius in education the South has ever produced. He lighted one generation and has since shamed the rest.

Possibly the most remarkable thing in Waddel's life was his students' definite, strong feeling for him--so strong unfortunately that they almost buried the real man forever in rhetoric eulogies, and provincial piety. There is no word in the English language to describe the feeling shared by the good teacher and the pupils he has helped to develop. "Love" is passion that smoulders and flames with envy, jealousy, and possessiveness. "Friendship" does not fit either; friendships are the result of mutual needs that change. "Appreciation" is too cold a word, and "gratitude" does not imply a time when personalities touched. It must suffice to say that between the student and the teacher there is a shared moment when the teacher's hope becomes the student's reality, when the realization they have been working for comes true, when they momentarily touch to share a common vision of a subject like history, chemistry, or literature. It is a moment of glory and communication which they have been working for, but a moment tinged with sadness because it signals that the time to part is near because the work has been achieved.

The student will always remember the teacher whose discipline enlarged him or whose mind brought him up a step. They may rarely see each other in later years and the feeling may be unexpressed because there is no word for it, but it is always in the back of the mind. The student remembers nostalgically the youthful rapture of communication, as if it had never taken place before, and smiles at the long-gone young self that, as he looks back, he realizes was such an idiot. The teacher will always feel as if he created a butterfly, which is not true, because the teacher is simply that spirit of nature which urges out whatever potential is in the "cocoon."

People do not have instincts such as other creatures have. Although nature will force the butterfly out of the cocoon, humanity has no such guaranteed instinct. Potential must be drawn out by teachers, who take the place with students that nature does with butterflies. Teachers represent the spirit of nature and urge the potential out of the young. Because the spirit of nature is behind them, even very commonplace people can do great things as teachers if they work, push, discipline, know their material and can be genuinely concerned. There can be no better proof of this than Moses Waddel.

ALUMNI FOREWORD

Waddel Academies

The first fifty short biographies are students Waddel taught in his various academies or who were at Willington when he was head of it. After Waddel returned to Willington from the University of Georgia, the main teaching at Willington was done by his sons, James and John, but Moses Waddel was still head of the academy. This sort of situation had existed at Willington before the Doctor went to the University of Georgia. It was not unusual at any time for him to delegate the teaching. The important thing is that under James and John the methods of their father's system were still continued. Students at Willington until the year 1836 are counted as orthodox Willington students.

Most of Waddel's alumni are not known. Few records have survived. Many were lost in the War for Southern Independence. Also in enumerating Waddel's alumni, people have tended to mention only famous political figures. An effort has been made to include ministers, medical doctors, planters, lawyers and others to have a more representative sampling.

Two worthies said to have gone to school to Waddel have been dropped because present available information does not seem to justify their inclusion. The two dropped are William H. Harper, a United States Senator from South Carolina and W. J. Grayson, Congressman and biographer of James Louis Petigru. It is also hoped this list will help to clear up some confusion as to the identity of some Waddel students. Margaret Coit in her aritcle on Waddel says he taught Howell Cobb, but it was Thomas Cobb. Other sources assert that he taught Jim Bowie of knife fame. It was actually Alexander Bowie, a Chancellor of Alabama 1839-1845.

University of Georgia

The University of Georgia did leave catalogues and yearly lists, but the list of those matriculating prior to 1821 has been lost and the lists extant are not complete. For example, Francis W. Pickens, governor of South Carolina 1860-62 who attended the University of Georgia before transferring to the University of South Carolina and dropping out in his senior year in 1827 is not mentioned. Therefore, not all students under Dr. Waddel are entered below.

Some few attended Willington and the University of Georgia, such as Charles Jones Jenkins and John A. Calhoun. These are in the Waddel Academy list.

In the list of forty Franklin College alumni from the Waddel period, an asterisk signifies a graduate of Franklin College under Waddel. No asterisk signifies a student at Franklin College who did not graduate under Waddel.

It should be remembered the names Franklin College and the University of Georgia were used synonymously at the time. The first building of the University of Georgia was called Franklin College in honor of Benjamin Franklin, so that young men were sent to Franklin College of the University of Georgia.

John H. Gray and James C. Patterson were Presbyterian ministers who read theology at Willington. Waddel, in the absence of seminaries had students came to take theology under him.

FIFTY WADDEL ACADEMY ALUMNI

1. Appling, Daniel (1787-1817) - Hero of the War of 1812. A native of Columbia County, Georgia, he enlisted in the U.S. Army in 1805. At the battle of Sandy Creek on Lake Erie in 1814 Major Appling with 130 of the Rifle Regiment and an equal number of Indians ambushed the British so successfully they surrendered in ten minutes. The spoils were three gunboats and several smaller vessels fully equipped. Made Lt. Colonel. In the attack on Plattsburg, Colonel Appling and his few riflemen and Indians held 14,000 British in check and then, led by Appling, made a daring and determined charge. British General Provost, demoralized at the news of a naval defeat, fled before Appling's brave few. Appling became a national hero. The legislature of Georgia placed Appling's sword in the Governor's Office "as a lasting memorial of his fame." In 1880 the sword was transferred to the Georgia Historical Society.

2. Bonham, Milledge Luke (1813-90) - Brigadier-general in the Confederate Army involved in the fighting around Fairfax, Centerville, Vienna, and First Manassas; elected to Confederate Congress in 1862 and in same year elected Confederate governor of South Carolina; resumed his generalship in 1865. Commander of S. C. Brigade in Seminole Indian Wars' Lieutenant-Colonel, 12th Infantry, Mexican War. Cited for conspicuous service in Mexican War by his commander, General (later President) Franklin Pierce. Member United States House of Representatives from 1857 until secession of South Carolina in 1860. Elected to Congress to fill unexpired term of his deceased cousin, Preston Smith Brooks. Mayflower descendant.

3. Bowie, Alexander (1789-?) - Chancellor of Alabama 1839-45; Trustee of the University of Alabama. Graduated from South Carolina College in 1809 where he was roommate of James Louis Petigru. Admitted to the S. C. Bar 1813. Member of S. C. House of Representatives 1818. Moved to Alabama in 1835 and was elected Chancellor of Northern Division of Alabama.

4. Boyce, William Waters (1818-1890) - Member U.S. House of Representatives from South Carolina 1853-61. Appointed delegate for South Carolina to Provisional Confederate Congress in 1861. Member Confederate Congress 1862-64. Moved Washington, D.C. in 1866 where he practiced law.

5. Brooks, Preston Smith (1819-57) - Member of the U.S. House of Representatives from South Carolina 1853-57. Brooks was a controversial figure. On May 20, 1856, Senator Charles Sumner of Massachusetts gave a violent, provocative, and ungentlemanly speech in the Senate. He mentioned by name in highly unfavorable terms an absent senator, Brooks' cousin, A. P. Butler of South Carolina, also a Willington alumnus. (The Dictionary of American Biography errs when it says A. P. Butler was Brooks' uncle. Brooks' father, Whitefield Brooks, and Andrew Butler were first cousins.)

Brooks demanded an apology from Sumner and received none. Angered at this denunciation of an absent kinsman, Brooks went to seek Sumner to "punish him." The Senate was adjourned but Sumner was still in his desk. To punish Sumner Brooks beat him on the head with a hollow walking cane until the cane broke. Brooks then left Sumner, whom he believed unconscious, on the floor of the Senate chamber.

A vote to expel Brooks from the House failed to receive a two-thirds vote. Brooks resigned anyway and was re-elected unanimously by his South Carolina constituency. Both Sumner and Brooks became regional heroes. Brooks was presented with many gold-headed canes to honor his whipping of the abolitionist for his poor manners. Brooks was presented with at least one gold handled cowhide whip.

When Brooks was a student at Dr. Waddel's, he "endeared himself to every boy...by his manly and generous qualities of character" according to his death notice. (For further exposition the October, 1978, South Carolina Historical Magazine carries an article, "Preston Smith Brooks: The Man and His Image" by Robert Neil Mathis.)

6. Butler, Andrew Pickens (1796-1857) - U.S. Senator from South Carolina 1846-57; Chairman of Senate Judiciary Committee 1849; Court of Appeals Judge 1833-46; Circuit Judge 1833; Trustee of South Carolina College (University of S.C.). Butler's speech on the Kansas-Nebraska bill was answered by Sumner's vituperative attack on May 20, 1856.

7. Butler, Pierce Mason (1799-1847) - Governor of South Carolina 1836-38; President of the Bank of South Carolina; Trustee of South Carolina College (University of S.C.); Organizer and Colonel of the Palmetto Regiment in the Mexican War, he was distinguished for bravery at the battle of Cerro Gordo and killed in the battle of Churubusco while leading his regiment against "one of the most terrific fires

to which soldiers were ever subjected." In 1838 he was an Indian agent praised by an Indian journal for being just and showing sympathy with the Cherokees. He was the younger brother of Senator Andrew Pickens Butler.

8. Calhoun, John Alfred (1807-1874) - President, Savannah River Railroad; Trustee, University of the South; Delegate to Secession Convention; State Representative; Mayor of Eufaula, Alabama. Large planter of "Rosdu" plantation, 135 slaves.

9. Calhoun, John Caldwell (1782-1850) - Vice-President of the U.S. 1825-32; Secretary of State 1843-45; Secretary of War 1817-25; U.S. Senator from South Carolina 1832-45; member U.S. House of Representatives from South Carolina 1811-17. Author. Political theorist.

10. Cary, George (1789-1843) - Member United States House of Representatives from Georgia, 1823-27. He was the editor of the Hickory Nut. Died in Upson County, Georgia.

11. Cobb, Thomas W. (1784-1830) - United States Senator from Georgia, 1824-28; member of U.S. House of Representatives from Georgia, 1817-24. Judge of Superior Court of Georgia. His epitaph reads, "As a statesman, independent, and inflexible. As a Judge, pure and incorruptible."

12. Colcock, William Ferguson (1804-1889) - Member of the U.S. House of Representatives from South Carolina 1849-53; Speaker of the S.C. House of Representatives 1841-47; Collector of the Port of Charleston; Trustee, South Carolina College (University of S.C.); Regent, Smithsonian Institution, Washington, D.C.; President, McPhersonville, S.C., Education Society. Large planter of Charleston and "The Ocean" plantation, 171 slaves. Authored two publications.

13. Collier, Henry Watkins (1801-55) - Alabama District Judge 1828-36; Associate Justice Alabama Supreme Court 1836-37; Chief Justice Alabama Supreme Court 1837-39; Governor of Alabama 1849-53.

14. Crawford, George Walker (1798-1872) - U.S. Secretary of War 1849-50; Governor of Georgia 1843-47; member U.S. House of Representatives from Georgia to fill vacancy 1/7-3/3/1843; Attorney-General of Georgia 1827-31; Chairman of Georgia Convention to secede in 1861. Robert Toombs said of him, "There are but few abler and no purer men in America, and he has administrative qualities of an unusually high order." He was second cousin to W. H. Crawford.

15. Crawford, William Harris (1772-1834) - U.S. Senator from Georgia 1807-13; President pro tempore 1812; U.S. Secretary of War, 1815-16; Secretary of the Treasury, 1816-25; minister to France, 1812-13; Democratic candidate for President of the U.S., 1824. Crawford's diary while in France has been printed in the Smith College Studies in History, Vol. XI, No. 2 (1925) edited by D. C. Knowlton.

16. Curry, Jabrz Lamar Monroe (1925-1930) - Member, U.S. House of Representatives from Alabama, 1857-61; member, Confederate Congress from Alabama, 1861-65; Lt. Colonel of Confederate Cavalry, 1864-65; President, Howard College, 1866-68; U.S. Minister to Spain, 1885-88; Board of Trustees, Richmond College; President, Southern History Association; First General Agent of the Peabody Endowment Fund and of John F. Slater Endowment Fund. Author: <u>Protestantism, How Far a Failure</u>, 1870; <u>History of the Peabody Endowment Fund</u>, 1898; <u>Civil History of the Confederate Government</u>, 1901.

17. Daniell, William Coffee (1792-1848) - Medical Doctor. Received M.D., 1815 from University of Pennsylvania; Mayor of Savannah; Editor of the <u>Savannah Republican</u>; correspondent, Elliott Society of Natural History; large planter of "Oglethorpe" plantation, 120 slaves. Authored several medical publications.

18. Dawson, Laurence E. (1799-1848) - a distinguished lawyer of South Carolina and Alabama, where he moved in 1842. His 1828 prosecution against a person for excessive cruelty to a slave was considered a "masterpiece of eloquence distinguished for richness of language, weight and solidity of argument, and a solemnity and vehemence of style." Mr. Dawson was "little in political life; having the good sense to see the futility of a service so dependent upon the voice of a changeable mob." He was considered an outstanding orator and "no one could see him without feeling that he was in the presence of a finished gentleman." He was considered a "perfect model" of the "high-tones, elevated and accomplished advocate."

19. Gibert, James Finlay (1808-1883) - Presbyterian minister; B. A. University of Georgia, 1834; B. D., Columbia Theological Seminary 1837; minister (half time) for Lebanon Congregation, Abbeville County, South Carolina 1838-1879; Liberty congregation in New Bordeaux settlement (part time) 1837-42; Hopewell Congregation, 1851-75 (part time). Also missionary work at the "County Poor House" 1852-79; licensed by Presbytery of South Carolina, 1837. Owner 29 slaves. Grandson of Pierre Gibert.

20. Gibert, John Albert (1821-92) - Medical doctor. Practiced nearly 40 years in Abbeville County, South Carolina. Original member of Huguenot Society of South Carolina, in which he was a first Vice-President. Owned "Orange Hill" plantation and 37 slaves. His tombstone in Old Willington Churchyard reads: "A Worthy Scion of That Devoted Huguenot Race Who Forsook Their Native France For the Sake of Jesus Christ. He lived a Busy Useful Life and Sleeps with His Fathers." Grandson of Pierre Gibert.

21. Gibert, Joseph Bienaime, Sr. (1790-1828) - Medical doctor. Practiced in Old Abbeville District, South Carolina, where his house was on Rocky River. A copy of Virgil's Bucolics read at Willington, now in the Caroliniana Library at the University of South Carolina, has his name in it. Son of Pierre Gibert who helped bring Waddel to Willington.

22. Gibert, Joseph Bienaime, Jr. (1817-1883) - Presbyterian minister. B.A., Franklin College (University of Georgia); B.D., Columbia Seminary, Columbia, S.C., 1844. Minister, Crawford County, Ga., 1844-49; congregation of Rock Run and Providence, Abbeville District, S.C., 1852-59; Covington County, Mississippi, 1859-1882. In April 1882 the cyclone which destroyed Monticello, Mississippi, "swept away his house, and rendered his little farm worthless." He died at his son's at Goalman, Mississippi. Grandson of Pierre Gibert.

23. Gilmer, George Rockingham (1790-1850) - Governor of Georgia 1828-31, 1837-39; member United States House of Representatives from Georgia 1821-23, 1826, 1833-35. Trustee of the University of Georgia. He left to the University of Georgia the Gilmer Fund for the training of teachers. Author: Sketches of Some of the First Settlers of Upper Georgia. In Sketches Gilmer revealed the truth of behind-the-scene details of his early associates in government. The book upset enough prominent families that attempts were made to buy and destroy the entire first edition.

24. Gray, John Hannah, D.D. (1804-78) - President, LaGrange College, Georgia 1857-62; Presbyterian minister; to Mesopotamia and Bethsalem churches, Greene County, Alabama, 1828-41; Jasper County, Mississippi, churches, 1841-43; Vicksburg, Mississippi, Church 1843-45; Second Church, Memphis, Tenn., 1845-47; First Secretary Presbyterian General Assembly on Education 1861-62.

25. Grier, Isaac, D.D. (1776-1843) - Presbyterian minister of the Associate Reformed Synod; B.D., Dickinson College, Pennsylvania, 1800; licensed at Long Cane,

South Carolina, September 2, 1802; minister of Sardis A.R.P. Church, Mecklenburg County, North Carolina, 1804-42; D.D., Jefferson College, Pennsylvania, 1837. First Presbyterian minister born in Georgia (Greene County).

26. Hillhouse, Joseph (1789-1855) - Studied theology at Willington under Dr. Waddel. Ordained in South Carolina Presbytery at his first pastorate, Fair Forest Church in 1817. He also served Bethel Church near Walhalla, South Carolina, and Union Church (formerly Brown's Creek), Bradaway, Varennes and Little Mountain Church. He married Harriet Gibert, daughter of Pierre Gibert.

27. Humphreys, David (1793-1869) - Presbyterian missionary to the Creek and Chickasaw Indians, 1820; minister, Good Hope and Roberts churches, South Carolina, 1821-42; minister, Anderson Church, Anderson, S.C., 1842-45; licensed by South Carolina Presbytery, 1819. Also served as a teacher for a time. Taught John Newton Waddel, Moses' son, how to read. Was considered a family friend of the Waddels.

28. Hunter, John S. (?-after 1865) - Circuit Judge in Alabama. Presided over the Whig Mass Convention at Tuskaloosa, Alabama, June 1840. "He was a gentleman of large wealth, and supported a liberal style, inclining somewhat to aristocratic notions, though he was usually social and courteous to all who approached him.... He was a fine scholar, and a smooth, pleasant speaker, his words falling like liquid pearls from his lips" (William Garrett, Reminiscences of Public Men in Alabama, 1872).

29. Jenkins, Charles Jones (1805-1883) - Governor of Georgia, 1865-68; removed for refusing to comply with the Reconstruction Acts of 1867. Speaker of the Georgia House of Representatives, 1840, 1843, 1847. Elected Attorney-General of Georgia, 1831. Justice, Supreme Court of Georgia, 1860-65. In 1850 offered post of Secretary of the Interior of the United States but declined. Went to Willington and then entered University of Georgia, transferred to Union College, New York where he graduated 1822. Admitted to Georgia Bar 1826.

    Jenkins was last governor to occupy the historic Old Governor's mansion in Milledgeville. Three of the eight governors who occupied it were Waddel students (Gilmer, G. W. Crawford, Jenkins), including the first (Gilmer) and last (Jenkins).

30. Jones, Noble Wymberly, II (1781-1818) - Son of Dr. George Jones of "Wormsloe" plantation, Georgia.

Married Sarah Campbell, his stepsister. Moved to
Philadelphia. Died there, predeceasing his father.

31. Legare, Hugh Swinton (1797-1843) - One of two editors
of Southern Review, 1828-32; Attorney-General of
South Carolina, 1830; U.S. House of Representatives
from South Carolina, 1837-39; United States Attorney-
General, 1841-43; U.S. Secretary of State (interim),
1843; U.S. Charge d'affaires in Belgium, 1832-36.
Author: Writings of Hugh Swinton Legare. Renowned
classical scholar.

32. Legare, Thomas (1795-1855) - Medical doctor. Received
M.D., University of Pennsylvania, 1818. South
Carolina Justice of the Quorum; local Commissioner
of Free Schools. Large planter of "Light House
Point" plantation and Johnstonville, owned 148 slaves.

33. Longstreet, Augustus Baldwin (1790-1870) - Circuit
Judge of Superior Court of Georgia, 1822-25; ordained
Methodist minister, 1838; president, Emory College,
1839-48; Centenary College at Jackson, Louisiana,
1849; University of Mississippi, 1849-56; University
of South Carolina, 1857. Author: Georgia Scenes,
Letters from Georgia to Massachusetts, Letter to
Clergymen of Northern Methodist Church, Master William
Mitten.

34. Martin, William Dobbins (1789-1833) - Member, United
States House of Representatives from South Carolina,
1827-31; Judge, Circuit Courts of Law and Appeal.
Martin attended Litchfield (Conn.) Law School. He
died in Charleston, S.C., and is buried in St.
Michael's church cemetery.

35. McDuffie, George (1790-1851) - Governor of South
Carolina, 1834-36; United States Senator from South
Carolina, 1842-46. Member, U.S. House of Representa-
tives, 1821-34; chairman, Ways and Means Committee,
1825-29. Large planter. Owner, "Cherry Hill"
Plantation, 202 slaves.

36. Miles, James Warley (1818-1875) - Anglican clergyman;
originator of the plan for the establishment of what
is now the Nashotah House Seminary in Wisconsin;
missionary to Mesopotamia, 1843-45; Constantinople,
1845-47; rector of St. John's Church, Johns Island,
South Carolina, 1847-49, but resigned because he
did not feel he could write a good sermon every
week. Professor of South Carolina College (University
of South Carolina), 1850-54; Librarian, South Carolina
College, 1856-62; Professor of Ancient Languages,
1865-71. He seems to have been a brilliant and
unusual clergyman. He wrote..."The Religious world
is unable to conceive a position not identified with

some party or school; and therefore they look upon me as an unsafe and dangerous person, not to be trusted with religious teaching, because my position is unintelligible to them, and I do not use the technical jargon or the dead cant of their systems."

37. Miles, William Porcher (1822-1899) - Member, U.S. House of Representatives from South Carolina, 1857-60. Chairman of the Committee on Foreign Relations of the South Carolina secession convention. One of three who arranged the terms of surrender of Fort Sumter. Mayor of Charleston, 1855-58, he represented Charleston in the Confederate Congress during its entire existence. Chairman of the Committee that devised the Confederate flag. Chairman of the important Committee on Military Affairs. President of the University of South Carolina, 1880-82. Moved to Louisiana in 1882, where he became a sugar planter, controlled thirteen plantations that produced twenty million pounds of sugar yearly. He had elegant manners, a handsome appearance, and a reputation for learning.

38. Morton, Augustus Hawkins (1817-1886) - Baptist deacon. Large planter of South Carolina; owner of "Oakwood" plantation, 170 slaves.

39. Noble, Patrick (1787-1840) - Governor of South Carolina, 1838-40. Speaker of the South Carolina House of Representatives, 1818-24, 1833-38. Early law partner of John C. Calhoun. Commissioner for railroad from Charleston to Cincinnati. Trustee of South Carolina College (University of South Carolina). Graduated from Princeton, 1806. Chancellor Bowie of Alabama, a friend, said of Noble: "His mind was rather more practical than brilliant. He had little imagination but a retentive memory. He was a well-read lawyer, and, without brilliant parts, he was a safe counsellor. He was one of the most amiable men I have every known."

40. Palmer, Edward Gendron (1800-1867) - President, Charlotte and South Carolina Railroad. Justice of the Peace; State Senator; State Representative; local Commissioner of Free Schools; Board of Visitors, Mount Zion schools. Large planter of "Valencia" plantation, owned 156 slaves.

41. Patterson, James Cowan (1803-1866) - President, Presbyterian Synod Female College of Georgia, Griffin, Ga., 1855-66; minister, Presbyterian Church in the United States (Southern), Milledgeville and Macon, Georgia, churches 1828-?; Fairview Church, Lawrenceville, Ga., 1839 and 1844; Goshen, Georgia, Church, 1851-55; ordained by Hopewell Presbytery, 1828.

42. Petigru, James Louis (1789-1863) - Lawyer and Attorney-General of South Carolina, 1822-30. He ran on Union ticket for U.S. Senate and lost in 1830. He disliked politics but took part because of a feeling that he had to in time of national crisis. He opposed the secession of South Carolina bitterly. Petigru was called the greatest private citizen South Carolina ever produced. Lincoln considered him for a Supreme Court Justice but declined because of his age. He codified all the state laws of South Carolina in Civil War years, paid by the legislature to reduce them to "exactness, precision and perspicuity."

43. Richardson, John Peter (1801-1869) - Governor of South Carolina, 1840-42; Member, U.S. House of Representatives from S.C., 1836-39; delegate to Southern Convention, 1850; member of Southern Rights Convention of 1852; member of South Carolina Secession Convention, 1860-62; signer of the Ordinance of Secession.

44. Screvan, James Proctor (1799-1859) - Medical doctor; received M.D. in 1820 from University of Pennsylvania and studied in Europe until 1822. He settled in Savannah, Georgia. Acting Mayor during the yellow fever epidemic of 1849, when every member of the city council except Screven and one other caught the disease. President of two railroads of great service in the development of the state, Savannah, Albany and Gulf R.R. and Atlantic and Gulf R.R., later consolidated into Savannah, Florida and Western R.R. Elected mayor of Savannah in 1856. He was "willing to put in superhuman labor to achieve his purpose." Large planter of "Screven's Ferry" plantation, owner 200 slaves.

45. Simkins, Eldred (1779-1831) - Member, United States House of Representatives from South Carolina, 1818-21; Lieutenant-governor of South Carolina, 1812-14. He attended the Litchfield (Conn.) Law School and was admitted to the bar in 1805. He was a lawyer and planter.

46. Telfair, Thomas (1780-1818) - Member of U.S. House of Representatives from Georgia, 1813-17. Graduated Princeton, 1805. Son of Governor Edward Telfair, first governor of Georgia by new Georgia Constitution of 1789-93. Thomas' death at 38 was considered to have cut off a promising career. Buried in Bonaventure Cemetery, Savannah.

47. Walker, John Williams (1782-1823) - United States Senator from Alabama, 1819-22; Speaker, Territorial House of Representatives, 1817; President, Alabama Constitutional Convention, 1819. One of first U.S. Senators from Alabama.

48. Wardlaw, David Lewis (1799-1873) - Law Judge of South Carolina, 1841-65; Associate Judge of the South Carolina Court of Appeals, 1865-68; Speaker of the South Carolina House of Representatives, 1836-41; Trustee of South Carolina College (University of South Carolina), 1836-68. Delegate to the State Convention of 1853, 1860-2, and September 1865. Admitted to the South Carolina Bar, 1830.

49. Wardlaw, Francis Hugh (1800-1861) - Chancellor of South Carolina, 1850-59; Judge of the South Carolina Court of Appeals, 1859-61; one of principal authors of South Carolina Ordinance of Secession. Admitted to South Carolina Bar, 1822; editor of Edgefield, S.C., newspaper, 1829-32. Brother of D. L. Wardlaw.

50. Wilson, John S. (1796-1873) - 1864 Moderator of General Assembly of Presbyterian Church in the United States (Southern); Stated Clerk of Presbyterian Synod of Georgia, 1871-72; first minister of Decatur, Georgia, Church, 1844-59; first minister and founder of First Church, Atlanta, Georgia, 1859-73; licensed by South Carolina Presbytery, 1819.

FORTY WADDEL UNIVERSITY OF GEORGIA ALUMNI

1. *Barnard, John Bradley (1897-61) - Lawyer and planter of Liberty County, Georgia. His obituary in the Savannah Republican reads, "Intelligent and well-informed, a gentleman by nature and education." Trustee of University of Georgia.

2. *Campbell, John Archibald (1811-89) - Associate Justice of U.S. Supreme Court, 1853-1861. In 1862 became Confederate Assistant Secretary of War. He entered Franklin College at eleven and graduated at fourteen. Upon his appointment to the Supreme Court he emancipated all his slaves.

3. *Chandler, Daniel (?-1866) - Solicitor-General of the Northern Georgia Circuit, 1831-38. His speech in 1835 at the University of Georgia published in 5,000 copies by admirers and said to have inspired founding of first female college in Goergia (Wesleyan). Moved to Alabama, where he became member of legislature.

4. *Chester, Norman L., M.D. (1803-76) - General practitioner in Gainesville, Georgia, 1830-37; Marietta, Goergia, 1837-76. Studied at Yale before entering Franklin College (University of Georgia).

5. *Crawford, Nathanial Macon (1811-71) - Son of Senator W. H. Crawford, who also studied under Waddel. Ordained Baptist minister, 1844. President, Mercer University, 1854-56, 1858-65; President, Georgetown College, Kentucky, 1865-71. Minister, First Baptist Church of Charleston, 1846-47.

6. *Cuyler, John M. (1810-84) - Entered army as Assistant Surgeon in 1834. Served in Creek War, 1838; Seminole War, 1840; Mexican War, 1846. Promoted to Major and Surgeon, 1847. Surgeon at West Point, 1848-55. Senior Medical officer at Fort Monroe in the Civil War. Brevetted Brigadier-General, Union Army, March 13, 1865.

7. *Doughtry, Robert (?-1868) - Judge of Northern Alabama Circuit, 1850-65. "He could keep a circle of friends in a constant roar of laughter for hours at a time. His stories were his own, told in his own way, and admit no transfer to paper." Became an alcoholic ("his downward course...was rapid").

8. *DuBignon, Charles (1809-76) - Graduated Yale Law College. Represented Glynn County, Georgia, in legislature. Captain in Cobb's Legion in the Confederate Army. Planter; married Ann Grantland,

well known in Milledgeville, old state capital, as "Old Miss." When Mrs. DuBignon arrived at one reception, the maid ran to tell the hostess, "Come, quick. Queen Victory done arrived."

9. *Eve, Paul Fitzsimons, M.D. (1806-87) - Surgeon. Credited with being the first American surgeon to perform a hysterectomy. President of American Medical Association, 1857-58. Chief surgeon of General Joseph E. Johnston's Confederate Army. Taught at various medical schools. Co-editor of Southern Medical and Surgical Journal. Myopic and tone deaf, he triumphed through methodical industry. Author of medical articles.

10. *Foster, Nathaniel Greene (1809-69) - Captain of a company in the Seminole War; U.S. Representative from Georgia, 1855-57; minister, Madison (Ga.) Baptist Church, 1855-69; Circuit Judge, 1867-68.

11. *Goulding, Francis R. (1810-1880) - Inventor of an early model sewing machine; author of children's classic, The Young Marooners. Presbyterian minister; promoted religious work among seamen of Charleston as agent of the Seamen's Friend Society.

12. *Haralson, Hugh Anderson (1805-54) - U.S. Congressman from Georgia, 1843-51; major-general, Georgia militia, 1838-50.

13. *Harris, Sampson Willis (1809-1857) - U.S. Congressman from Alabama, 1847-57. Declined to be candidate for renomination in 1856.

14. *Harris, William L. (?-?; class of 1825) - "After establishing at the bar his wide reputation as a great thinker and debater, he was first judge of the circuit court, and then removed to Supreme Court bench" of Mississippi (Reuben Davis, Recollections of Mississippi and Mississippians, 1889). Harris was disqualified as judge by the Reconstruction government in 1867.

15. *Hillyer, Junius (1807-1886) - Circuit Judge in Georgia, 1841-45; U.S. House of Representatives from Georgia, 1851-55; Solicitor of the U.S. Treasury, 1857-61.

16. *Holt, Hines (1805-65) - U.S. Representative from Georgia, 1840; First Confederate Congress, 1862-64; died attending as delegate State Constitutional Convention at Milledgeville, 1865.

17. *Jones, William E. (?-?; class of 1826) - Lawyer, editor; delegate to Congress of Republic of Texas

from Gonzales; Chairman of House Foreign Relations Committee. Called "Fiery" Jones of Gonzales. He was also a District Judge (resigned 1842) who, according to law of nation, served as an Associate Justice of its supreme court.

18. Lamar, John Basil (1812-62) - U.S. Congressman from Georgia, 1843; trustee of Univeristy of Georgia, 1855-58. Delegate to the State Convention which adopted the Secession Ordinance; Colonel, C.S.A., killed in battle at Crampton's Gap, Md. His plantation extended throughout central and southwest Georgia and into Florida.

19. Lumpkin, John H. (1812-1860) - U.S. Congressman from Georgia, 1843-49, 50-53. Judge of the Superior Court, 1850-53.

20. Meek, Alexander Beaufort (1814-65) - Lawyer, newspaper editor, author. U.S. attorney for Southern District of Alabama, 1846-50. Associate Editor of Mobile Daily Register, 1848-53. Chairman of Legislative Committee on Education that recommended Alabama establish and maintain a public school system. Appointed Judge, Mobile City Court, 1851. Wrote Songs & Poems of the South. His poem "Land of the South" set to music.

21. *Meriwether, James A. (1806-52) - Judge of Georgia Superior Court, 1845-49; U.S. House of Representatives from Georgia, 1841-43; Speaker, Georgia House of Representatives, 1852.

22. *Mitchell, William Letcher (1805-82) - Professor of Law and trustee of the University of Georgia. A. L. Hull said: "Mr. Mitchell might be called intense. He was positive in every phase of his character--a warm friend, a bitter enemy.... He hated the Yankees and despised every church but the Presbyterian. He was naturally dogmatic." Waddel performed his marriage to Sarah Neisler on December 25, 1828.

23. *Newton, Elizur Lawrance (1796-1882) - Athens, Georgia, merchant. Built first brick building in Athens. Owner Newton Hotel. Son of Rev. John Newton, pioneer Presbyterian minister who organized first Georgia Presbytery along with Moses Waddel and others.

24. *Nisbet, Eugenius Aristides (1803-1871) - Admitted to the bar by special act of legislature before he was 21. U.S. Congressman from Georgia, 1839-41; Associate Judge of Supreme Court of Georgia, 1845-53. Member of Secession Convention of Georgia in 1861 and was author of the ordinance of secession.

25. Norwood, James Alexander (1810-1874) - Large planter of "White Lick" plantation, Abbeville District, South Carolina. Owned 196 slaves.

26. Pickens, Francis Wilkinson (1807-69) - Governor of South Carolina, 1860-62. Succeeded Bonham. Studied law, married daughter of law partner, Eldred Simkins. U.S. House of Representatives, 1834-43, succeeding McDuffie; U.S. minister to Russia, 1858-60. Pickens authorized first military action of Civil War when South Carolina troops fired on the ship, Star of the West.

27. *Pierce, George Foster (1811-1884) - Bishop of Methodist Church, South. President of Georgia Female College (Wesleyan), 1838-40; president of Emory College, 1848-54. Elected bishop, 1854. Lived at "Sunshine" plantation near Sparta, Georgia.

28. *Pinney, John (18 -18) - Presbyterian minister, first Presbyterian missionary to West Africa (Liberia) in 1833.

29. Safford, Joseph P. (?-1853) - Chancellor of Southern Division of Alabama, approximately 1850-53. Died of yellow fever. Son of Judge Reuben Saffold. Governor Collier of Alabama said on Joseph's death, "He was a man of great purity of character, and admirably adapted, by his attainment and the structure of his mind, to the station to which he had been called."

30. *Scott, Thomas Fielding (1807-1867) - Anglican bishop. First missionary bishop of Oregon and Washington Territory. Licensed to preach in the Presbyterian Church, he converted to Anglicanism in 1842. Went in 1854 to Oregon, where his pioneer hardships earned him the reputation of an American martyr.

31. Shields, Benjamin Glover (1808-died after 1850) - U.S. House of Representatives from Alabama, 1841-43; U.S. Charge' d' Affaires to Venezuela, 1845-50.

32. Stephens, Alexander Hamilton (1812-1883) - Vice-President of the Confederacy. U.S. House of Representatives from Georgia, 1843-59; member, Secession Convention of Georgia, 1861, opposed secession; U.S. Representative from Georgia, 1873-1882; governor of Georgia, 1882 until death in 1883. Imprisoned in Fort Warren, Boston, for five months in 1865. Author.

33. Stoney, Peter Gaillard (1809-84) - Large planter of "Medway" plantation (Back River), South Carolina.

He and six sons fought with the Confederacy. Grandson of Captain Peter Gaillard, one of first Southern planters to grow cotton successfully on a large scale. Owner of 120 slaves.

34. Toombs, Robert (1810-1885) - Secretary of State of the Confederacy; Brigadier-General, C.S.A.; U.S. Representative from Georgia, 1845-53; U.S. Senator from Georgia, 1853-61. Expelled by vote of faculty from University of Georgia under Waddel but finished college at Union College, New York, and University of Virginia.

35. *Waddel, Isaac Watts, D.D. (1804-49) - Son of Moses Waddel. He was a Presbyterian minister who served churches at Willington, S.C.; Demopolis, Alabama; and Marietta, Georgia. His son, James Daniel Waddel, cooperated with Alexander Stephens to write the biography of Linton Stephens, Alexander's brother. Isaac Watts was licensed in 1828, ordained 1829.

36. *Waddel, James Pleasants (?-1867) - Son of Moses Waddel. He was a Professor of Classical Languages in Franklin College. He was an elder in the Athens Presbyterian Church. His son, William Henry Waddel, was a Professor of Greek at the University of Georgia.

37. *Waddel, John Newton (1812-1895) - Son of Moses. Presbyterian minister. Established Montrose Academy, Miss., in 1842, a school similar to Willington. President, LaGrange College, 1860-62. Chancellor of University of Mississippi, 1865-74; Southwestern University, 1879-1888. First Stated Clerk of Presbyterian Church U.S., 1861-65. Moderator of General Assembly, 1868. Author.

38. *Waddel, William Woodson (?-1843) - Son of Moses Waddel. He was a physician who practiced in Athens, Georgia, and removed for health reasons to Tallahassee, Florida, where he died. He was an elder in the Presbyterian Church of Tallahassee.

39. Wellborn, Marshall Johnson (1808-1874) - Judge of Superior Court of Georgia, 1838-42; U.S. Representative from Georgia, 1849-51. Ordained Baptist minister, 1864.

40. Wright, Augustus Romaldus (1813-1891) - Judge of the Superior Court, 1842-49; U.S. Congressman from Georgia, 1857-59; delegate to Georgia Secession Convention, opposing secession; member, Confederate Congress; organized Wright's Legion, part of 38th Georgia Infantry, C.S.A.

I.

OLD MOSES

1. William B. Sprague. Annals of the American Pulpit (Robert Carter & Brothers, New York, 19858), IV, 65.

2. George R. Gilmer. Sketches of Some of the First Settlers of Upper Georgia (Genealogical Publishing Co., Baltimore, 1965), p. 185.

3. George Howe. History of the Presbyterian Church in South Carolina (Columbia, S.C.: W. J. Duffie, 1883), II, 541.

4. R. J. Calhoun and J. C. Guilds. A Tricentennial Anthology of South Carolina Literature, 1670-1970 (Columbia: University of South Carolina Press, 1971), pp. 182-83.

5. Sprague, p. 66.

6. William J. Grayson. James Louis Petigru (New York: Harper & Brothers, 1866), p. 34.

7. John N. Waddel. Memorials of Academic Life (Richmond, Va.: Presbyterian Committee of Publications, 1891), p. 94.

II.

AN AMERICAN ETON

1. McDuffie: Butler, P. M.; Noble; Richardson. Noble died in office and the Lieutenant Governor served until the election of Richardson.

2. Noble; Wardlaw, D. L.; Colcock.

3. McDuffie; Butler, A. P.; Calhoun, J. C.

4. Bonham; Boyce; Brooks; Calhoun, J. C.; Cary; Colcock; Govan; Legare, H.; Martin; McDuffie; Miles, W. P.; Richardson; Simkins.

5. Martin, 1830; Butler, A. P., 1833; Wardlaw, D. L., 1841.

6. Petigru, 1822; Legare, H., 1830.

7. Wardlaw, F. H. (Judge, Court of Equity); Petigru (U.S. Attorney for S.C.).

8. Butler, P. M.

9. Palmer (Charlotte & S.C.R.R.); Calhoun, J. A. (Savannah Rivery Valley R.R.).

10. Miles, W. P. (Charleston); Screven (Savannah).

11. Wardlaw, F. H.

12. Longstreet, A. B.

13. Two senators: Cobb, T. W.; Crawford, W. H.
    Five congressmen: Cary; Cobb, T. W.; Crawford, G. W.; Gilmer; Telfair
    Three governors: Crawford, G. W.; Gilmer; Jenkins

14. Governor: Collier
    Senator: Walker
    Chief Justice, Alabama Supreme Court: Collier
    Chancellor: Bowie
    Representative: Curry

15. Bonham (S.C.); Butler, P. M. (S.C.); Collier (Ala.); Crawford, G. W. (Ga.); Gilmer (Ga.); Jenkins (Ga.); McDuffie (S.C.); Noble (S.C.); Richardson.

16. Calhoun, J. C.; Crawford, G. W.; Crawford, W. H.

17. Calhoun, J. C., 1843-45
    Legare, H., 1843 (ad interim)

18. Crawford, W. H.

19. Calhoun, J. C.

20. Appling (War of 1812); Butler, P. M. (Mexican War).

21. Congressmen: Bonham; Boyce; Curry; Miles, W. P.; Waters
    Governor: Bonham (S.C.)
    Brigadier-General: Bonham

22. Calhoun, J. C.; Cary; Colcock; Crawford, W. H.; Curry; Daniell; Gilmer; Legare, H.; Longstreet; Miles, J. W.; Petigru; Wardlaw, F. H.

23. Curry (Howard); Gray (LaGrange); Longstreet (Emory, Centenary, Univ. of Mississippi, Univ. of S.C.); Miles, W. P. (Univ. of S.C.); Patterson (Presbyterian Synod Female College of Georgia).

24. John Belton O'Neall. *Biographical Sketches of the Bench and Bar of South Carolina* (Charleston, S.C.: S. G. Courtenay and Co., 1859), II, 392.

25. *Ibid.*

26. William J. Northern. *Men of Mark in Georgia* (Spartanburg, S.C.; The Reprint Co., 1974), II, 227.

III.

FRANKLIN COLLEGE, UNIVERSITY OF GEORGIA

1. Stephens

2. Toombs

3. Foster; Haralson; Hillyer; Holt; Lamar; Lumpkin; Meriwether; Stephens; Toombs; Wellborn; Wright.

4. Pickens

5. Harris, S.; Shields

6. Campbell; Doughtry; Foster; Harris; Hillyer, J.; Jones, W. E.; Lumpkin, J. H.; Meek; Meriwether; Nisbet; Saffold; Wellborn; Wright.

7. Crawford; Pierce; Waddel

8. Chandler; Eve; Goulding; Meek; Stephens; Waddel

9. Campbell

10. Pickens

11. Eve

12. Scott

13. Pierce

14. Listed in italics in University of Georgia Catalogue lists contained in Augustus L. Hull, *A Historical Sketch of the University of Georgia* (Atlanta: Foote Davis Co., 1894).

15. Meek

16. Stephens

17. Toombs

18. Campbell

19. Wright

20. Toombs

21. Jones, W. E.

22. Cuyler

23. Calhoun, J. C. ; Stephens
24. Calhoun, J. C.; Legare, H.; Toombs
25. Calhoun, J. C.; Crawford, G. W.; Crawford, W. H.
26. Campbell
27. Legare, H.
28. France: Crawford, W. H.
    Spain: Curry
    Russia: Pickens
29. Campbell
30.
    1. Bonham   - S.C.
    2. Butler, P. M.   - S.C.
    3. Collier   - Ala.
    4. Crawford, G. W. - Ga.
    5. Gilmer   - Ga.
    6. Jenkins   - Ga.
    7. McDuffie   - S.C.
    8. Noble   - S.C.
    9. Pickens   - S.C.
    10. Richardson   - S.C.
    11. Stephens   - Ga.
31.
    1. Butler, A. P.   - S.C.
    2. Calhoun, J. C.   - S.C.
    3. Cobb, T. W.   - Ga.
    4. Crawford, W. H.   - Ga.
    5. McDuffie   - S.C.
    6. Toombs   - Ga.
    7. Walker   - Ala.
32.
    1. Bonham   - S.C.
    2. Boyce   - S.C.
    3. Brooks   - S.C.
    4. Calhoun, J. C.   - S.C.
    5. Cary   - Ga.
    6. Cobb, T. W.   - Ga.
    7. Colcock   - S.C.
    8. Crawford, G. W. - Ga.
    9. Curry   - Ala.
    10. Foster   - Ga.
    11. Gilmer   - Ga.
    12. Haralson   - Ala.
    13. Harris, S. W.   - Ga.
    14. Hillyer   - Ga.
    15. Holt   - Ga.
    16. Lamar   - Ga.
    17. Legare, H. S.   - S.C.
    18. Lumpkin, J. H.   - Ga.
    19. Martin   - S.C.

	20.	McDuffie	- S.C.
	21.	Meriwether	- Ga.
	22.	Miles, W. P.	- S.C.
	23.	Nisbett	- Ga.
	24.	Pickens	- S.C.
	25.	Richardson	- S.C.
	26.	Shields	- Ala.
	27.	Simkins	- S.C.
	28.	Stephens	- Ga.
	29.	Telfair	- Ga.
	30.	Toombs	- Ga.
	31.	Wellborn	- Ga.
	32.	Wright	- Ga.
33.	1.	Bowie	- Chancellor, Ala.
	2.	Butler, A. P.	- Court of Appeals, Circuit, S.C.
	3.	Campbell	- U.S. Supreme Court
	4.	Cobb	- Superior Court, Ga.
	5.	Collier	- Chief Justice, Alabama Supreme Court
	6.	Doughtry	- Circuit, Ala.
	7.	Foster	- Circuit, Ga.
	8.	Harris, W. L.	- Supreme Court, Mississippi
	9.	Hillyer	- Circuit, Ga.
	10.	Hunter	- Circuit, Ala.
	11.	Jenkins	- Supreme Court, Ga.
	12.	Jones	- District Judge, Texas
	13.	Longstreet	- Circuit, Ga.
	14.	Lumpkin	- Superior Court, Ga.
	15.	Meek	- Mobile, Ala. City Court
	16.	Meriwether	- Superior Court, Ga.
	17.	Nisbett	- Supreme Court, Ga.
	18.	Saffold	- Chancellor, Ala.
	19.	Wardlaw, D. L.	- Law Judge; Court of Appeals, S.C.
	20.	Wardlaw, F. H.	- Chancellor; Court of Appeals, S.C.
	21.	Wellborn	- Superior Court, Ga.
	22.	Wright	- Supreme Court, Ga.
34.	1.	Crawford, N. M.	- Mercer Univ., Ga.; Georgetown College, Ky.
	2.	Curry	- Howard College
	3.	Gray	- LaGrange College, Ga.
	4.	Longstreet	- Emory Univ., Ga.; Centenary, La.; Univ. of Miss.; Univ. of S.C.
	5.	Miles, W. P.	- Univ. of S.C.
	6.	Patterson	- Presbyterian Synod Female College, Griffin, Ga.
	7.	Pierce	- Emory Univ., Ga.
	8.	Waddel, J. N.	- LaGrange College, Ga.; University of Miss.
35.	1.	Calhoun, J.C.	
	2.	Cary	

3. Colcock
4. Chandler
5. Crawford
6. Curry
7. Daniell, W. C.
8. Eve
9. Gilmer
10. Goulding
11. Legare, H. S.
12. Longstreet
13. Meeks
14. Petigru
15. Stephens
16. Waddel, J. N.
17. Wardlaw, F. H.

36. Bonham; Boyce, W. W.; Curry; Miles, W. P.; Holt

37. Scott   - Anglican bishop of Oregon
    Fielding   - Methodist bishop of Georgia

38. Bonham (C.S.A.)
    Cuyler (Union)
    Toombs (C.S.A.)

39. According to the Dictionary of American Biography, Thomas Fielding Scott, Anglican bishop of Oregon and Washington Territory, endured pioneer hardships that earned him the reputation of an authentic martyr.

IV.

THE SCOTCH-IRISH

1. James G. Leyburn, The Scotch-Irish (Chapel Hill: University of North Carolina Press, 1976), p. 139.

2. Ibid., p. 153.

3. Virginius Dabney, Liberalism in the South (Chapel Hill: University of North Carolina Press, 1932), p. 43-44.

4. Ralph M. Lyon, "Moses Waddel and the Willington Academy," North Carolina Historical Review, Vol. no. (July 1931), 285.

5. George Howe, History of the Presbyterian Church in South Carolina (Columbia, S.C.: I. Duffie & Chapman, 1870), p. 442-443.

6. Look to the Rock, (Richmond, Va.: John Knox Press, 1961), p. 120.

7. George Gilmer, Sketches of Some of the First Settlers of Upper Georgia (Baltimore; Genealogical Publishing Co., 1970), p. 185.

8. Leyburn, P. 323.

V.
BORN

1. John Newton Waddel, Memorials of Academic Life (Richmond, Va: Presbyterian Committee of Publication, 1891), p. 26.

2. Edward G. Lilly, Beyond the Burning Bush (Charleston, S.C.: Garnier and Co., 1971), pp. 58-59.

3. John N. Waddel, p. 26.

4. Ibid., pp. 26-27.

5. Ibid., pp. 27-28.

6. Ernest T. Thompson, Presbyterians in the South (Richmond, Va.: John Knox Press, 1963) I, 94-95.

7. John N. Waddel, p. 28.

8. Thompson, p. 95.

9. George Howe, History of the Presbyterian Church in South Carolina (Columbia, S.C.: Duffie and Chapman, 1870) I, 632.

10. Thompson, p. 245.

11. "The Waddel Memoir," Georgia Historical Quarterly, VIII (Dec. 1924), 308.

12. John N. Waddel, p. 29.

13. "The Waddel Memoir," p. 309

14. Ibid.

15. Ibid.

VI.

BORN AGAIN

1. "The Waddel Memoir," Georgia Historical Quarterly, VIII (December, 1924), 309.

2. W. B. Sprague, Annals of the American Pulpit (New York: Arno Press and the New York Times, 1969), IX, 110.

3. "The Waddel Memoir," p. 310.

4. Ibid., p. 311.

5. Ibid., p. 313.

6. Ibid., p. 316.

7. Ibid., p. 316.

8. Ibid., pp. 318-319.

9. Ibid., pp. 321-322.

10. Ibid., p. 322.

11. Ibid., p. 322.

12. Franklin C. Talmage, The Story of the Synod of Georgia (Atlanta: Privately published by Presbyterian Synod of Georgia, 1961), p. 21.

13. William Wirt, The Letters of the British Spy (Chapel Hill: University of North Carolina Press, 1970), p. 200.

VII.

HAMPDEN-SYDNEY

1. Alfred J. Morrison, *The College of Hampden-Sydney: Calendar of Board Minutes 1776-1876* (Richmond, Va.: The Hermitage Press, 1912), pp. 12-13.

2. Ernest Trice Thompson, *Presbyterians in the South* (Richmond, Va.: John Knox Press, 1963), I, 82.

3. Ibid., p. 59.

4. A. Johnson and D. Malone, *Dictionary of American Biography* (New York: Charles Scribner's Sons, 1936_, IX, 299.

5. Thompson, p. 127.

6. Jonathan Edwards, *Edwards on Revivals* (New York: Dunning & Spalding, 1832), p. 60.

7. Ibid., p. 105.

8. Thompson, p. 129.

9. Ibid., p. 142.

10. "The Waddel Memoir," *Georgia Historical Quarterly*, VIII (December, 1924), 323.

11. Letter from the Rev. Drury Lacy, dated February 20, 1793, Col. Watkins', Charlotte, Virginia, Waddel Papers, Library of Congress.

12. *Look to the Rock* (Richmond, Va.: John Knox Press, 1961), p. 124.

13. Thompson, p. 257.

14. Moses Waddel Diary, May 16, 1836, Waddel Papers, Library of Congress.

VIII.

THE LOW COUNTRY

1. George Howe, History of the Presbyterian Church in South Carolina (Columbia, S.C.: Duffie and Chapman, 1870) I, 653.

2. A Tricentennial Anthology of South Carolina Literature (Columbia: University of South Carolina Press, 1971), pp. 186-87.

3. Howe, p. 653.

4. Paul McIlvaine, The Dead Towns of Sunbury and Dorchester, Published by Paul M. McIlvaine, Route 3, Box 90, Hendersonville, N.C. 28739, Groves Printing Co., Asheville, N.C., c 1971, p. 69.

5. R. M. Myers, The Children of Pride (New Haven, Conn.: Yale University Press, 1973), pp. 7-8.

6. Joseph Belcher, George Whitefield (New York: American Tract Society), p. 465.

7. Ibid., p. 198.

8. Belcher, p. 362.

9. Ibid., pp. 206-207.

10. John N. Waddel, Memorials of Academic Life (Richmond, Va.: Presbyterian Committee of Publication, 1891), pp. 65-66.

11. Letter of John Walker to Moses Waddel, dated January 19, 1806, Nassau Hall, Waddel Papers, Library of Congress.

12. Letter of Thomas Legare to Moses Waddel, dated September 29, 1796, Charleston, S.C., Waddel Papers, Library of Congress.

13. Letter of Thomas Legare to Moses Waddel, dated March 6, 1798, Charleston, S.C., Waddel Papers, Library of Congress.

IX.

CARMEL

1. Francis Cummins, The Spriitual Watchman's Character, Call and Duty Described (Charleston, S.C.: Markland & M'Iver, 1795), pp. 18-19.

2. George Howe, History of the Presbyterian Church in South Carolina (Columbia, S.C.. W. J. Duffie, 1883), II, 145.

3. Franklin C. Talmage, The Story of the Synod of Georgia (Atlanta, Ga.: Privately printed by Presbyterian Synod of Georgia, 1961), p. 30.

4. A. Johnson and D. Malone, eds., Dictionary of American Biography (New York: Charles Scribner's Sons, 1936), II, 528.

5. F. Tupper and J. W. Tupper, eds., Representative English Dramas from Dryden to Sheridan (New York: Oxford University Press, 1934), p. 376.

6. Ibid., p. 374.

7. Douglas MacMillan and Howard M. Jones, eds., Plays of the Restoration and Eighteenth Century (New York: Henry Holt & Co., c 1931), p. 517.

8. J. E. D. Shipp, Giant Days (Americus, Ga.: Southern Printers, 1909).

9. Tupper and Tupper, pp. 378-403.

10. Atlanta, Ga. Constitution, March 18, 1934.

11. Josephine Mellichamp, Senators from Georgia (Huntsville, Ala.: Strode Publishers, Inc., c 1976), p. 25.

12. Ibid., p. 65.

13. Margaret Coit, John C. Calhoun (Boston: Houghton Mifflin Co., 1950), p. 126.

X.

MARRIAGE

1. George Howe, History of the Presbyterian Church in South Carolina (Columbia, S.C.: Duffie & Chapman, 1870) I, 64-65.

2. Ibid., p. 655.

3. John N. Waddel, Memorials of Academic Life (Richmond, Va.: Presbyterian Committee of Publications, 1891), pp. 47-48.

4. Margaret Coit, John C. Calhoun (Boston: Houghton, Mifflin Co., 1950), pp. 7-8.

5. R. W. Simpson, History of Old Pendleton District (S.C.) (Covington, Tenn.: Bradford Publishing Co., 1913 reprint) pp. 140-144, 189, 196.

6. The Story of Washington-Wilkes (Athens: University of Georgia Press, 1941) p. 111.

7. Howe, II, 142-143.

8. Coit, pp. 6-7.

9. Ibid., p. 48.

10. John N. Waddel, p. 119.

11. Augustus L. Hull, Annals of Athens, Georgia, 1801-1901 (Athens, Ga.: Banner Office, 1906), pp. 475-6.

XI.

WILLINGTON

1. George Howe, History of the Presbyterian Church in South Carolina (Columbia, S.C.: Duffie and Chapman, 1870), I, 442-43.

2. Mary E. Moragne, The Neglected Thread (Columbia: University of South Carolina Press, 1951), p. XVII.

3. W. E. Hemphill, ed., The Papers of John C. Calhoun (Columbia, S.C.: University of South Carolina Press, 1969), IV, 492.

4. Augustus B. Longstreet, Master William Milten (Macon: Burke, Boykin & Co., 1864), p. 86.

5. Ibid., p. 164.

6. Augustus B. Longstreet, Eulogy on the Life and Services of the Late Rev. Moses Waddel, D.D. (Augusta, Ga.: 1841), p. 7.

7. George Gilmer, Sketches of Some of the First Settlers of Upper Georgia (Baltimore: Genealogical Publishing Co., 1965), pp. 184-185.

8. Letter from Col. Thomas Taylor to the Rev. Moses Waddel dated Dec. 18, 1803, Waddel papers, Library of Congress.

9. John Donald Wade, Augustus Baldwin Longstreet: A Study of the Development of Culture in the South (New York: The Macmillan Co., 1924), p. 29.

10. Longstreet, Master William Milten, p. 81.

11. Ibid.

12. William J. Grayson, James Louis Petigru, A Biographical Sketch (New York: Harper & Brothers, 1866), p. 34.

XII.

FREEDOM AND JUSTICE FOR ALL

1. R. J. Calhoun and J. C. Guilds, eds., A Tricentennial Anthology of South Carolina Literature, 1670-1970 (Columbia, S.C.: University of South Carolina Press, 19), p. 185.

2. A. B. Longstreet, Master William Mitten (Macon, Ga.: Burke, Boykin & Co., 1864).

3. Ibid., p. 75.

4. Ibid., p. 78.

5. Ibid.

6. Ibid., p. 79.

7. John N. Waddel, Memorials of Academic Life (Richmond, Va.: Presbyterian Committee of Publication, 1891), p. 57.

8. Calhoun & Guilds, p. 187.

9. George R. Gilmer, Sketches of Some of the First Settlers of Upper Georgia (Baltimore: Genealogical Publishing Co., 1970), p. 181.

10. Ibid.

11. "Sam Houston Taught Here," Southern Living 13 (No. 10, October, 1978), 18.

12. David Ramsay, History of South Carolina (Newberry, S.C.: W. J. Duffie, 1858), 206.

13. Longstreet, pp. 81-86.

XIII.

TEACHER

1. W. B. Sprague, Annals of the American Pulpit (New York: Robert Carter and Bros., 1858), IV, 67.

2. Hugh S. Legare, Writings, ed. Mary S. Legare (Charleston: Publ. Co., 1846), I, XV.

3. R. J. Calhoun and J. C. Guilds, eds., A Tricentennial Anthology of South Caroline Literature 1670-1970 (Columbia: Pub., 1971), p. 124.

4. A. Johnson and D. Malone, eds., Dictionary of American Biography (New York: Charles Scribner's Sons, 1927), II, 528.

5. Letter from John Walker to Moses Waddel, dated January 19, 1806, Nassau Hall. Waddel Papers, Library of Congress.

6. David Ramsay, History of South Carolina (Newberry, S.C.: W. J. Duffie) II, 371.

7. Sprague, IV, 66.

8. William J. Grayson, James Louis Petigru, A Biographical Sketch (New York: Harper and Brothers, 1866), p. 33.

9. Letter from Ruben Langston, to Moses Waddel, dated March 6, 1806. Columbia County, Goergia, Waddel Papers, Library of Congress.

10. Letter from John B. Posey to Moses Waddel, dated July 22, 1805. Nassau Hall, New Jersey, Waddel Papers, Library of Congress.

11. Letter from Moses Waddel to George Jones, dated Dec. 15, 1798, Columbia Academy. Southern Historical Collection, Chapel Hill, North Carolina.

12. A. L. Hull, Annals of Athens, Goergia 1801-1901 (Athens, Ga.: Job Banner Office, 1906), p. 57.

XIV.

CURRICULUM

1. George Howe, History of the Presbyterian Church in South Carolina (Columbia, S.C.: W. J. Duffie, 1885), II, 542.

2. Colyer Meriwether, History of Higher Education in South Carolina (Washington, D.C.: Government Printing Office, 1889), p. 40.

3. David Ramsay, History of South Carolina (Newberry, S.C.: W. J. Duffie, 1848), II, 206.

4. Meriwether, p. 37.

5. Meriwether, p. 40.

6. Letter from John Walker to Moses Waddel, dated December 10, 1805, Nassau Hall, Waddel Papers, Library of Congress.

7. John Furman Thomason, Foundation of the Public Schools in South Carolina (Columbia, S.C.: Pub. Co., 1925), pp. 99-100.

8. A. B. Longstreet, Master William Mitten (Macon, Ga.: Burke, Boykin & Co., 1864), pp. 72-73.

9. Meriwether, p. 42.

10. A. B. Longstreet, Georgia Scenes, Characters, Incidents (Savannah, Ga.: The Beehive Press, 1975), pp. 152-168.

11. William M. Meigs, The Life of John Caldwell Calhoun (New York: G. E. Stechert & Co., 1917), I, 66.

12. Longstreet, Georgia Scenes, p. 152.

13. Daniel Walker Hollis, South Carolina College (Columbia: University of South Carolina Press, 1951), I, 260.

14. George Howe, History of the Presbyterian Church in South Carolina (Columbia, S.C.: W. J. Duffie, 1883), II, 541.

15. Ibid.

16. Hollis, P. 261.

17. Ibid., p. 260.

18. James G. Leyburn, The Scotch-Irish (Chapel Hill: University of North Carolina Press, 1962), p. 324.

19. Margaret Coit, *John C. Calhoun* (Boston: Houghton-Mifflin Co., 1950), p. 62.

20. *Ibid.*, p. 393.

21. *Ibid.*, p. 396.

22. Leyburn, p. 324.

23. *Ibid*, pp. 324-25.

24. Clement Eaton, *The Growth of Southern Civilization, 1790-1860* (New York: Harper & Row, 1961), p. 115.

25. "The Correspondence of John C. Calhoun," *Fourth Annual Report of the Historical Manuscripts Commission of the American Historical Association* (Washington, D.C.: Pub. Co., 1900), p. 79.

XV.

LEADERS FROM THE WOODS

1. A. B. Longstreet, Eulogy on the Life and Public Services of the Late Rev. Moses Waddel, D.D. (Augusta, Ga.: Chronicle & Sentinel Co., 1841), p. 15.

2. Edwin Green, George McDuffie (Columbia, S.C.: The State Company, 1936), p. 12.

3. Report of the Commissioner of Education, (Washington, D.C.: Government Printing Office, 1895-96), I, 289.

4. David Ramsay, History of South Carolina (Newberry, S.C.: W. J. Duffie, 1858), IV, 66.

5. W. B. Sprague, Annals of the American Pulpit (New York: Robert Carter & Brothers, 1858), IV, 66.

6. A. B. Longstreet, Master William Mitten (Macon, Ga.: Burke, Boykin, & Co., 1864), p. 98.

7. W. J. Grayson, James Louis Petigru (New York: Harper & Brothers, 1966), p. 33.

8. V. L. Parrington, The Romantic Revolution in America, 1800-1860 (New York: Harcourt, Brace & Co., 1927), p. 115.

9. R. J. Calhoun and J. C. Guilds, eds., A Tricentennial Anthology of South Carolina Literature, 1670-1970 (Columbia: University of South Carolina Press), p. 132.

10. Ibid., p. 133.

11. Ibid., p. 125.

12. Parrington, p. 124.

13. Margaret L. Coit, John C. Calhoun, (Boston: Houghton Mifflin Co., 1950), p. 505.

14. Ramsay, pp. 208-9.

XVI.

CROMWELL OF THE CLASSROOM

1. George Howe, History of the Presbyterian Church in South Carolina (Columbia, S.C.: W. J. Duffie, 1883), II, 143.

2. Ibid., p. 144.

3. R. J. Calhoun and J. C. Guilds, eds., A Tricentennial Anthology of South Carolina Literature, 1670-1970 (Columbia: University of South Carolina Press, 1971), p. 187.

4. Ibid.

5. Ibid.

6. Howe, p. 144.

7. Ibid.

8. William B. Sprague, Annals of the American Pulpit (New York: Robert Carter and Bros., 1858), IV, 66.

9. "The Waddel Memoir," Georgia Historical Quarterly, VIII (Dec. 1924), 316.

10. A. B. Longstreet, Master William Mitten (Macon, Ga.: Burke, Boykin & Co., 1864), p. 75.

11. Hugh S. Legare, Writings of Hugh Swinton Legare (Charleston, S.C.: Buyes and James, 1846), I, xviii-xix.

12. Longstreet, p. 80.

13. John N. Waddel, Memorials of Academic Life (Richmond, Va.: Presbyterian Committee of Publication, 1891), pp. 57-58.

14. David Ramsay, History of South Carolina (Newberry, S.C.: W. J. Duffie, 1858), II, 206-7.

15. Howe, p. 543.

XVII.

COMMENCEMENT AND COLLEGE

1. Daniel Walker Hollis, South Carolina College (Columbia: University of South Carolina Press, 1951), I, 39.

2. Letter from Jonathan Maxcy to the Rev. M. Waddel, dated, January 17, 1806, Columbia, S.C., Waddel Papers, Library of Congress.

3. Hollis, p. 40.

4. Letter from William James to Moses Waddel, dated June 18, 1806, Columbia, S.C., Waddel Papers, Library of Congress.

5. Robert L. Meriwether, ed., Papers of John C. Calhoun, 1801-1817 (Columbia: University of South Carolina Press, 1959), I, 38.

6. A. B. Longstreet, Master William Mitten (Macon, Ga.: Burke, Boykin & Co., 1864), p. 123.

7. Ibid., pp. 124-126.

8. Letter from John W. Walker to Moses Waddel, dated May 1, 1803, New Jersey Waddel Papers, Library of Congress.

9. Letter from John W. Walker to Moses Waddel, dated June 15, 1803, Nassau Hall, Waddel Papers, Library of Congress.

10. Letter from John B. Posey to Moses Waddel, dated October 7, 1805, Princeton, Waddel Papers, Library of Congress.

11. Letter from John B. Posey to Moses Waddel, dated July 22, 1805, Nassau Hall, Waddel Papers, Library of Congress.

12. Letter from John B. Posey to Moses Waddel, dated October 7, 1805, Princeton, Waddel Papers, Library of Congress.

13. Letter from John B. Posey to Moses Waddel, dated April 24, 1806, Princeton. Waddel Papers, Library of Congress.

XVIII.

DECISIONS, DECISIONS

1. William M. Meigs, The Life of John Caldwell Calhoun (New York: G. E. Stechert & Co., 1917), I, 83.

2. William B. Sprague, Annals of the American Pulpit (New York: Robert Carter & Brothers, 1858), IV, 70.

3. Ibid., p. 68.

4. A. B. Longstreet, Eulogy on the Life and Public Services of the Late Rev. Moses Waddel, D.D. (Augusta, Ga.: Chronicle and Sentinel Co., 1841), p. 16.

5. Ernest T. Thompson, Presbyterians in the South (Richmond, Va.: John Knox Press, 1963), I, 136.

6. John N. Waddel, Memorials of Acadmic Life (Richmond, Va.: Presbyterian Committee of Publication, 1891), p. 101.

7. Ibid., p. 69.

8. Ibid., p. 101.

9. Sprague, p. 68.

10. Ibid., p. 70.

11. George Howe, History of the Presbyterian Church in South Carolina (Columbia, S.C.: W. J. Duffie, 1883), II, 145.

12. Waddel, p. 101.

13. Ibid., p. 97.

14. Thompson, p. 82.

15. Longstreet, pp. 16-19.

16. Robert M. Goldenson, The Encyclopedia of Human Behavior (Garden City, N.Y.: Doubleday & Co., c 1970), I, 244-245.

17. Colyer Meriwether, History of Higher Education in South Carolina (Columbia, S.C.: Government Printing Office, 1889), p. 46.

18. Edwin Hemphill, ed., Papers of John C. Calhoun, 1819-20 (Columbia: University of South Carolina Press, 1969), IV, 492-93.

XIX.

THE UNIVERSITY OF GEORGIA

1. Merton E. Coulter, College Life in the Old South (Athens: The University of Georgia Press, c 1951), p. 218.

2. Minutes of the Senatus Academicus for November 30, 1799, Library, University of Georgia, Athens.

3. John N. Waddel, Memorials of Academic Life (Richmond, Va.: Presbyterian Committee of Publication, 1891), pp. 75-76.

4. Clement Eaton, The Growth of Southern Civilization (New York: Harper & Row, 1961), p. 161.

5. A. B. Longstreet, Eulogy on the Life and Public Services of the Late Rev. Moses Waddel, D.D. (Augusta, Ga.: Chronicle and Sentinel Co., 1841), p. 12.

6. Coulter, p. 34.

7. Diary of Moses Waddel, May 2, 1829, Waddel Papers, Library of Congress.

8. Coulter, p. 88.

9. John N. Waddel, p. 197.

10. George Gilmer, Sketches of Some of the First Settlers of Upper Georgia (Baltimore: Genealogical Publishing Co., 1970), p. 186.

11. Appleton's Cyclopedia of American Biography (New York: D. Appleton and Co., 1889), VI, 310.

12. Letter from Moses Waddel to Joseph V. Bevan, dated March 14, 1825, Athens. Southern Historical Collection, Chapel Hill, North Carolina.

13. Hugh S. Legare, Writings of Hugh Swinton Legare (Charleston, S.C.: Burges and James, 1846), I, xx.

XX.

MINISTER

1. Sermon Texts of Moses Waddel, 1819-1836, Waddel Papers, Library of Congress.

2. Diary of Moses Waddel, October 14, 1828, Waddel Papers, Library of Congress.

3. Diary of Moses Waddel, December 14, 1828, Waddel Papers, Library of Congress.

4. Diary of Moses Waddel, August 1, 1830, Waddel Papers, Library of Congress.

5. John N. Waddel, Memorials of Academic Life (Richmond, Va.: Presbyterian Committee of Publications, 1891), p. 198.

6. Diary of Moses Waddel, June 2, 1830, Waddel Papers, Library of Congress.

7. George Howe, History of the Presbyterian Church in South Carolina (Columbia, S.C.: W. J. Duffie, 1883), II, 541.

8. John N. Waddel, p. 196.

9. James G. Leyburn, The Scotch-Irish (Chapel Hill: University of North Carolina Press, 1976), p. 291.

10. Franklin C. Talmage, The Story of the Synod of Georgia (1961), pp. 24-25.

11. Howe, p. 291.

12. Ibid., p. 542.

XXI.

REVIVALISM AND THE COLLAPSE OF THE COVENANT

1. Penrose St. Amant, A History of the Presbyterian Church in Louisiana (Synod of Louisiana, 1961), p. 31.

2. John M. Bateman, First Presbyterian Churchyard (Privately printed pamphlet) p. 19.

3. Edward G. Lilly, Beyond the Burning Bush (Charleston, S.C.: Garnier 1971), p. 42.

4. Look to the Rock (Richmond, Va.: John Knox Press, 1961), p. 139.

5. Ibid., p. 129.

6. Ernest Trice Thompson, Presbyterians in the South, 1607-1861 (Richmond, Va.: Knox Press, 1963), I, 322.

7. Mary E. Moragne, The Neglected Thread (Columbia: University of South Carolina Press, 1951), p. 42.

8. John Newton Waddel, Memorials of Academic Life (Richmond, Va.: Presbyterian Committee of Publication, 1891), p. 55.

9. William B. Sprague, Annals of the American Pulpit (New York: Robert Carter and Brothers, 1858), IV, 59-60.

10. George Howe, History of the Presbyterian Church in South Carolina (Columbia, S.C., W. J. Duffie, 1883), II, 146.

11. Hull, pp. 53-54.

12. The New Psalms and Hymns (Richmond, Va.: Presbyterian Committee of Publications, 1901), p. 465, Hymn 579.

XXII.

THE DIVINE VISITATION

1. Jonathan Edwards, Edwards On Revivals (New York: Dunning & Spalding, 1832), pp. 87-88.

2. Ibid., pp. 94-96.

3. W. B. Sprague, Annals of the American Pulpit (New York: Robert Carter & Brothers, 1858), IV, 65.

4. Biographical Directory of the American Congress 1774-1971 (Washington, D.C.: U.S. Government Printing Office, 1971), p. 1709.

5. Moses Waddel, Memoirs of the Life of Miss Caroline E. Smelt (New York: D. Franshaw, 1819), p. 11.

6. Ibid., p. 15.

7. Ibid., p. 21.

8. Ibid., p. 39.

9. Ibid., p. 52.

10. Ibid., p. 58.

11. Ibid., p. 68.

12. Ibid., p. 74.

13. Ibid., p. 75.

14. Ibid., p. 155.

15. Ibid., pp. 166-167.

16. R. M. Lyon, "Moses Waddel and the Willington Academy," North Carolina Historical Review, Vol. (July 1931), 298.

17. Margaret L. Coit, John C. Calhoun (Boston: Houston-Mifflin Co., 1950), p. 508.

18. William M. Meigs, The Life of John Caldwell Calhoun (New York: G. E. Stechert & Co., 1917, I, 83.

XXIII.

THE CALVINIST PARADOX

1. Merton E. Coulter, College Life in the Old South (Athens: University of Georgia Press, 1951), p. 69.

2. George Howe, History of the Presbyterian Church in South Carolina (Columbia, S.C.: W. J. Duffie, 1883), II, 759.

3. Clement Eaton, The Growth of Southern Civilization (New York: Harper & Row, c 1961), p. 293.

XXIV.

PLANTATION LIFE

1. Charleston (S.C.)-Mercury, January 8, 1839.
2. Clement Eaton, The Growth of Southern Civilization (New York: Harper & Row, c 1961), p. 187.
3. John N. Waddel, Memorials of Academic Life, Presbyterian Committee of Publication, Richmond, Va., p. 190.
4. Ibid.
5. The (Athens, Ga.) Athenian, April 20, 1830.
6. Eaton, p. 31.
7. Ibid.
8. Waddel, p. 190.
9. Colyer Merwether, History of Higher Education in South Carolina (Columbia, S.C.: Government Printing Office, 1889), p. 44.
10. A. Johnson and D. Malone, eds., Dictionary of American Biography (New York: Charles Scribner's Sons, 1958), II, 605-06.
11. Eaton, p. 30.
12. Waddel, p. 185.
13. Sarah Blackwell Gober Temple, The First Hundred Years (Atlanta: W. Brown Publishing Co., 1935), p. 652.

XXV.

DANGERS AND DEPTHS

1. Diary of Moses Waddel, August 29, 1836, Waddel Papers, Library of Congress.

2. John N. Waddel, Memorials of Academic Life (Richmond, Va.: Presbyterian Committee of Publication, 1891), p. 125.

3. Ibid., p. 126.

4. George Howe, History of the Presbyterian Church in South Carolina (Columbia, S.C.: W. J. Duffie, 1883), II, 543.

5. Mary E. Moragne, The Neglected Thread (Columbia: University of South Carolina Press, 1951), pp. 44-45.

6. Charleston (S.C.)-Mercury, January 8, 1839.

7. Howe, p. 543.

8. John N. Waddell, p. 126.

9. Moragne, p. 159.

10. William B. Sprague, Annals of the American Pulpit (New York: Robert Carter & Brothers, 1858), IV, 70.

11. Diary of Moses Waddel, May 31, 1836, Waddel Papers, Library of Congress.

12. Moragne, p. 172.

BIBLIOGRAPHY

Books

Alderman, E. A. and Gordon, A. C. J. L. M. Curry. New York. 1911.

Allen, Alexander V. Jonathan Edwards. Saint Clair Shores, Missouri. 1976.

Appleton's Cyclopedia of American Biography, VI. New York. 1889.

Bailey, Hugh C. John Williams Walker. University, Alabama. 1964.

Barnhart, E. L. (ed.) New Century Handbook of English Literature. New York. 1956.

Belcher, Joseph. George Whitefield. New York. ca. 1850.

Biographical Directory of the American Congress, 1774-1971. Washington. 1971.

Biographical Directory of the Senate of the State of South Carolina 1776-1964.

Biographical Directory of the South Carolina House of Representatives, I. Columbia, S.C. 1974.

Blair, Hugh. Lectures on Rhetoric and Belles Letters, I. Boston. September 1802.

Boudinot, Elias. The Life of the Reverend William Tennent. Hartford. 1845.

Brooks, U. R. South Carolina Bench and Bar, two volumes. Columbia, S.C. 1908.

Carson, James Petigru. Life, Letters and Speeches of James Louis Petigru. Washington, D.C. 1920.

Cherry, Conrad, et al. Jonathan Edwards: His Life and Influence. Cranbury, N.J. 1975.

Clebceh, William A. American Religious Thought. (Chicago History of Religion Series) Chicago. 1973.

Cocks, H. Lovell. The Religious Life of Oliver Cromwell. Napierville, Ill. 1961.

Coit, Margaret C. John C. Calhoun. Boston. 1950.

Coulter, E. Merton. College Life in the Old South. Athens. c 1951.

172

Coulter, E. Merton. Wormsloe, Two Centuries of a Georgia Family. Athens, Ga. c 1955.

Dabney, Virginius. Liberalism in the South. Chapel Hill, 1932.

Dabney, Charles William. Universal Education in the South, I. Chapel Hill, 1936.

Davidson, Chalmers Gaston. The Last Foray. Columbia, S.C. 1971.

Davidson, Edward H. Jonathan Edwards: The Narrative of a Puritan Mind. Cambridge. 1968.

Davis, Arthur Paul. Isaac Watts: His Life and Works. New York. 1943.

Dictionary of American Biography. New York. 1936.

Eaton, Clement. The Growth of Southern Civilization, 1790-1860. New York. 1961.

Edwards, Jonathan. Edwards On Revivals. New York. 1932.

Fludd, Eliza C. K., Biographical Sketches of the Huguenot Solomon Legare and of His Family. Charleston. 1886.

Ford, Henry Jones. The Scotch-Irish in America. Princeton, N.J. 1915.

Gewehr, Wesley M. The Great Awakening in Virginia, 1740-1790. Durham, N.C. 1930.

Gibert, Anne Caroline. Pierre Gibert, Esq., The Devoted Huguenot. Published by the author, 1976.

Gilmer, George R. Sketches of Some of the First Settlers of Upper Georgia. Baltimore. 1965.

Glasgow, Maud. The Scotch-Irish in Northern Ireland and in the American Colonies. New York. 1936.

Goldenson, Robert M. The Encyclopedia of Human Behavior, I. New York. 1970.

Graydon, Nell S. Tales of Columbia. Columbia, S.C. 1973.

Grayson, W. J. Life of John C. Calhoun. Charleston. 1903.

Grayson, William J. James Louis Petigru. New York. 1866.

Green, Edwin. George McDuffie. Columbia, S.C. 1936.

Hall, Thomas Cumming. *The Religious Background of American Culture*. Boston. 1930.

Harden, E. J. *Life of George M. Troup*. Savannah. 1859.

Hemphill, W. E. (ed.) *The Papers of John C. Calhoun*, nine volumes. Columbia. 1969.

Hillhouse, Albert M. *Pierre Gibert, French Huguenot, His Background and Descendants*. Danville, Kentucky. c 1977.

Hillis, Newell D. *Great Men as Prophets of a New Era*. New York. 1968.

Hirsch, Arthur Henry. *The Huguenots of Colonial South Carolina*. Durham, N.C. 1928.

Hollis, Daniel Walker. *University of South Carolina, South Carolina College, I*. Columbia, 1951.

Howe, George. *History of the Presbyterian Church in South Carolina*, two volumes. Columbia, S.C. 1883.

Hull, Augustus L. *Annals of Athens, Georgia, 1801-1901*. Athens, Ga. 1906.

Hull, A. L. *A Historical Sketch of the University of Georgia*. Atlanta. 1894.

Hunt, Gaillard. *John C. Calhoun*. Philadelphia. 1908.

Jones, Charles Edgeworth. *Education in Georgia, No. 5*. Washington. 1889.

Johnson, Charles A. *The Frontier Camp Meeting*. Dallas. 1955.

King, Spencer B., Jr. *Georgia Voices: A Documentary History to 1872*. Athens, Ga. c 1966.

Kirbye, J. Edward. *Puritanism in the South*. Boston. 1908.

Knight, E. W. *The Academy Movement in the South*. Chapel Hill. 1919.

Knight, Edgar A. *Documentary History of Education in the South Before 1860, II and IV*. Chapel Hill. 1949.

Knight, Lucian Lamar. *Georgia's Landmarks, Memorials, Legends*. Atlanta. 1914.

Legare, Hugh S. *Writings of Hugh Swinton Legare*, two volumes. Charleston. 1846.

Leyburn, James G. The Scotch-Irish. Chapel Hill. 1976.

Library of Southern Literature, XV. Atlanta. 1910.

Lilly, Edward G. Beyond the Burning Bush. Charleston. 1971.

Longstreet, A. B. Georgia Scenes, Characters, Incidents. Savannah. 1975.

Longstreet, A. B. Master William Mitten. Macon, Georgia. 1864

Look To The Rock. Richmond, Virginia. 1961.

MacMillan, Douglas, & Jones, Howard (eds.). Plays of the Restoration and Eighteenth Century. New York. c 1931.

Mathews, Donald G. Religion in the Old South. Chicago. 1977.

McGiffert, Arthur C. Jonathan Edwards. New York. 1976.

McIlwaine, Henry Read. The Struggle of Protestant Dissenters for Religious Toleration in Virginia. Baltimore. 1894.

McIlvaine, Paul. The Dead Towns of Sunbury and Dorchester. Asheville, N.C. 1971.

Meigs, William M. The Life of John Caldwell Calhoun, two volumes. New York. 1917.

Mellichamp, Josephine. Senators from Georgia. Hunstville, Alabama. c 1976.

Memorial Volume of the Semi-Centennial of the Theological Seminary at Columbia, S.C. Columbia. 1884.

Meriwether, Colyer. History of Higher Education in South Carolina. Columbia, South Carolina. 1889.

Milledge, John. Correspondence of John Milledge. Columbia, S.C. 1949.

Miller, Howard. The Revolutionary College. New York. 1976.

Miller, Perry. Jonathan Edwards. Westport, Conn. 1973.

Ministerial Directory of the Presbyterian Church, U.S., 1861-1941. Austin, Texas. 1942.

Moragne, Mary E. The Neglected Thread. Columbia. 1951.

Moore, Arthur K. *The Frontier Mind*. Lexington, Kentucky. 1957.

Morrison, Alfred J. *The College of Hampden-Sydney: Calendar of Bd. Minutes 1776-1876*. Richmond. 1912.

Myers, R. M. (ed.). *The Children of Pride*. New Haven. 1973.

New, John F. (ed.). *Oliver Cromwell: Pretender, Puritan Statesman, Paradox?* Huntington, New York. 1976.

The New Psalms and Hymns. Richmond, Va. 1901.

Northern, William J. *Men of Mark in Georgia*, two volumes. Spartanburg, S.C. 1974.

O'Neall, John Belton. *Biographical Sketches of the Bench and Bar of South Carolina*, two volumes. Spartanburg, S.C. 1975.

Opie, John. *Jonathan Edwards and the Enlightenment*. Indianapolis. 1969.

Parrington, V. L. *The Romantic Revolution in America, 1800-1860*. New York. 1927.

Perry, Ralph Barton. *Puritanism and Democracy*. New York. 1944.

Phillips, U. B. *The Life of Robert Toombs*. New York. 1913.

Phillips, Ulrich B. *Life and Labor in the Old South*. Boston. 1963.

Pinckney, G. M. *Life of John C. Calhoun*. Charleston. 1903.

Pollocks, John. *George Whitefield and the Great Awakening*. Garden City, New York. 1972.

Ramsay, David. *History of South Carolina, II*. Newberry, S.C. 1858.

Report of the Commissioner of Education, I (1895-96). Washington.

Rhea, Linda. *Hugh Swinton Legare*. Chapel Hill. 1934.

Rice, Jessie Pearl. *J. L. M. Curry*. Columbia University. 1949.

Ross, Fred A. *Slavery Ordained by God*. Philadelphia. 1857.

Shaw, James. *The Scotch-Irish in History*. Springfield, Mass. 1899.

Shipp, J. E. D. *Giant Days*. Americus, Ga. 1909.

Simpson, Addison W. *Life and Service of Reverend John Springer*. 1941.

Simpson, R. W. *History of Old Pendleton District* (S.C.). Carrington, Tenn. 1913 reprint.

The South in the Building of the Nation, XII. Richmond, Va. 1909.

Sprague, William B. *Annals of the American Pulpit*, volumes III, IV, IX. New York. 1858.

St. Amant, Penrose. *A History of the Presbyterian Church in Louisiana*. Synod of Louisiana. 1961.

Stacy, James. *A History of the Presbyterian Church in Georgia*. Elberton, Ga. 1912.

Stephenson, George M. *The Puritan Heritage*. New York. 1952.

Stokes, Thomas L. *The Savannah (Rivers of America Series)*. New York. 1951.

Sweet, William Warren. *The Presbyterians*, II (Religion on the American Frontier 1783-1840). Chicago. 1936.

Talmage, Franklin C. *The Story of the Synod of Georgia*. 1961.

Taylor, R. H. *Ante-Bellum South Carolina*. Chapel Hill. 1942.

Temple, Sarah Blackwell Gober. *The First Hundred Years*. Atlanta. 1935.

Thompson, Ernest T. *Presbyterians in the South, I*. Richmond. 1963.

Thomason, John F. *Foundation of the Public Schools in South Carolina*. Columbia. 1925.

Tracy, Joseph. *Great Awakening: A History of the Revival of Religion in the Time of Edwards and Whitefield*. New York. Reprint of 1954 edition.

A Tricentennial Anthology of South Carolina Literature, 1670-1970. Columbia, S.C. 1971.

Tupper, F. and J. W. (eds.). *Representative English Dramas from Dryden to Sheridan.* New York. 1934.

Twelve Southerners. *I'll Take My Stand.* New York. c 1962.

Tyerman, Luke. *The Life of the Rev. George Whitefield.* New York. 1976.

Waddel, John N. *Memorials of Academic Life.* Richmond. 1891.

Waddel, Moses. *Memoirs of the Life of Miss Caroline E. Smelt.* New York. 1819.

Wade, John Donald. *Augustus Baldwin Longstreet.* New York. 1924.

Wallace, David Duncan. *History of South Carolina, II.* New York. 1934.

Whitefield, George. *The Work of Reverend George Whitefield,* six volumes. New York. 1976.

White, George, The Rev. *Historical Collections of Georgia.* New York. 1855.

White, Henry Alexander. *Southern Presbyterian Leaders.* New York. 1972.

Who Was Who in America, 1907-1896. Chicago. 1963.

Winslow, Ola E. *Jonathan Edwards, 1903-1758.* New York. 1972.

Wirt, William. *The Letters of the British Spy.* Chapel Hill. 1970.

Periodicals and Pamphlets

An Account Genealogical and Occasionally Somewhat Biographical of the Family of D. L. Wardlaw. Abbeville, S.C.: privately printed 1891.

Bailey, Hugh C. "The Petersburg Youth of John Williams Walker." Georgia Historical Quarterly, XLIII (June 1959), 123-37.

Bailey, Hugh C. "The Up Country Academies of Moses Waddel." Proceedings of the South Carolina Historical Association, 1956, pp. 36-43.

Bateman, John M. First Presbyterian Churchyard, Columbia, South Carolina. Privately printed pamphlets, 1920.

Burns, Martha Bailey (ed.). "Very Affectionately, H. S. Legare." Transactions of the Huguenot Society of South Carolina, No. 71 (1966), pp. 50-3.

Chaffin, J. E. "Address-Dedication of Willington Academy Marker." McCormick County Historical Society Transaction No. 1 (1971-72), McCormick, South Carolina, p. 11-16.

Corne, Donald R. "The Influence of Princeton on Higher Education in the South Before 1825." The William and Mary Quarterly, Third Series, II (1945), 359-396.

Coulter, E. M. "The Antebellum Academy Movement in Georgia." Georgia Historical Quarterly, Vol. 5, No. 4, December 1921, pages 11-45.

Craven, E. R. "The Log Cabin of Neshaminy and Princeton University." Journal of the Presbyterian Historical Society, I (1902), 314-25.

Cummins, Francis. The Spiritual Watchman's Character, Call and Duty Described. Charleston: Markland and M'Iver, 1795.

Green, Edward R. R. "The Scotch-Irish and the Coming of the Revolution in North Carolina." Irish Historical Studies, VII (Sept. 1950), 77-86.

Harrison, Lowell. "South Carolina's Educational System in 1822." The South Carolina Historical and Genealogical Magazine, LI (Jan. 1950), 1-9.

Jameson, J. Franklin (ed.). "Correspondence of John C. Calhoun." Annual Report of the American Historical Association, II (1899).

Lesesne, J. M. "The French Huguenot of New Bordeaux." <u>Transactions of the Huguenot Society of South Carolina</u>, No. 77 (1972), pp. 1-8.

Longstreet, Augustus B. <u>Eulogy on the Life and Public Service of the Late Rev. Moses Waddel, D.D.</u> Augusta: Ga.: Chronicle and Sentinel Co., 1841.

Lyon, Ralph M. "Moses Waddel and the Willington Academy." <u>North Carolina Historical Review</u>, Vol. No. 8 (July, 1931), pages 284-299.

McCully, Robert S. "Moses Waddel, Pioneer Pedagogue." <u>South Carolina History Illustrated</u>, Vol. I, No. I (Feb., 1970).

"Sam Houston Taught Here," <u>Southern Living</u>, 13, No. 10 (Oct., 1978), p. 18.

"The Waddel Memoir." <u>Georgia Historical Quarterly</u>, VIII (Dec., 1924), 304-24.

Williams, George. <u>The Reverend James Warley Miles</u>. Charleston, S.C.: Dalcho Historical Society, 1954.

Manuscripts

Bass, Robert D. (ed.). "The Autobiography of William J. Grayson." Unpublished Ph.D. dissertation, University of South Carolina, 1933.

Des Champs, Margaret Burr. "The Presbyterian Church in the South Atlantic States 1801-1861." Ph.D. thesis, Emory University, 1952.

J. L. M. Curry Papers. Library of Congress.

John W. Walker Papers. Alabama Department of Archives and History.

Knox, Paul. "The Development of Education in Abbeville County, South Carolina." Master's thesis, University of South Carolina, 1929.

Larkin Newby Collection. Duke University Library.

Moses Waddel Diary, January 1822 to September 1836, and other papers, Library of Congress.

Moses Waddel Letters, 1798-1825, Southern Historical Collection, University of North Carolina, Chapel Hill.

Senatus Academicus Minutes, 1799-1842. University of Georgia.

Walsh, Walter R. "Secondary Education in South Carolina, 1800-1801." Unpublished essay, South Carolinana Library, Columbia, S.C.

Willis, James Otis. "Moses Waddel and His Willington Academy." B.A. Thesis, University of South Carolina, 1936.

Newspapers

Abbeville (S.C.) Press and Banner, July 28, 1886.

The Athenian (Athens, Ga.), April 20, 1830.

The Atlanta Journal. March 18, 1934.

Augusta (Ga.) Chronicle, October 14, 1797; Sept. 28, 1799; April 23, 1796; Nov. 13, 1802; July 23, 1803.

Charleston (S.C.) Courier, May 24, 1810.

Charleston (S.C.)-Mercury, Jan. 8, 1839.

Georgia and Carolina Gazette (Petersburg, Ga.), July 25, 1805; July 24, 1806; June 5, 1806; Nov. 30, 1805.

The State (Columbia, S.C.), September 20, 1936.

INDEX
Compiled by
Ella E. Lee Sheffield

ADDISON, Joseph 34
ALLEN, Cary 23
APPLING, Lt. Colonel -- 127
  Major -- 127
  Daniel 127
ARNOLD, -- 4
  Dr. -- 3, 9
  Mrs. -- 116
  Thomas, Dr. 3, 8
BARNARD, John Bradley 137
BERKELEY, William, Sir 11
BEVAN, Joseph V. 88
BIBB, George M. 25
BONHAM, -- 140
  Milledge Luke 127
BOWIE, Alexander 6, 125, 127
  Chancellor 134
  Jim 125
BOYCE, William Waters 127
BROOKS, Preston Smith 127, 128
  Whitefield 128
BUCHAN, George, Rev. 98
BULL, John 114
  William, Lt. Gov. 41
BUTLER, A. P. 128
  Andrew 128
  Andrew Pickens 128, 129
  Pierce Mason 128
CALHOUN, -- 4, 55, 59, 64, 82, 110
  Catherine 36, 37, 38, 40, 119
  James 37
  John 36, 37, 38, 62
  John A. 8, 126
  John Alfred 129
  John C. 3, 4, 5, 8, 30, 35, 36, 38, 42, 43, 50, 59, 70, 79, 90, 92, 107, 118, 134
  John C., Jr. 118
  John Caldwell 129
  Kitty 36
  Martha 37
  Patrick 36, 37, 41, 62
  William 37
CALVIN, John 106, 108
CAMPBELL, -- 53
  Justice -- 8
  John Archibald 137
  Sarah 132
CAREY, George 56
CARY, George 129
CHANDLER, Daniel 137
CHESTER, Norman L. 137
CHURCH, Dr. -- 76
  Dr. Alonzo 75
CLAPP, Theodore 97
COBB, -- 137
  Howell 125
  Thomas 125
  Thomas W. 35, 80, 89, 129
CODNER, Elizabeth, Mrs. 102
COIT, -- 59
  Margaret 125
COLCOCK, William Ferguson 129
COLLIER, Miss -- 116
  Henry Watkins 129
COPPERFIELD, David 10
COULTER, -- 84
  E. M. 82

COULTER (cont.)
  E. M erton 35
CRAIG, Elijah, Rev. 24
CRAWFORD, -- 34, 82
  E. H. 62
  G. W. 132
  George Walker 129
  Nathanial Macon 137
  W. H. 33, 35, 89, 129, 137
  William H. 3
  William Harris 33, 130
CROMWELL, -- 10, 37
  Oliver 66
CROW, Jim 115
CUMMINGS, Francis 61
CUMMINS, Francis 17, 32
CUNNINGHAM, Captain -- 101
  Robert 101
CURRY, -- 115
  Jabez Lamar Monroe 114, 130
CUYLER, John M. 137
DANIELL, William Coffee 130
DAVIS, Reuben 138
DAWSON, Laurence E. 130
DOUGHTRY, Robert 137
DU BIGNON, Mrs. -- 138
  Ann Grantland 137
  Charles 137
EATON, Clement 59, 115
EDWARDS, -- 100, 104
  Jonathan 24, 28, 99, 101, 103, 105
EMERSON, -- 121
  Ralph Waldo 107
EVE, Paul, Dr. 7
  Paul Fitzsimons 138
FOSTER, Nathaniel Greene 138
FRANKLIN, Mrs. -- 101
  Benjamin 8
FREUD, Anna 2
GAILLARD, Peter, Capt. 141
  Theodore, Jun. 54
GARRETT, William 132
GIBERT, Harriet 132
  James Finlay 130
  John Albert 131
  Joseph Bienaime, Jr. 131
  Joseph Bienaime, Sr. 131
  Pierre 41, 42, 130, 132
GILES, Squire 116
GILMER, -- 132
  Gov. -- 3
  George 44, 48, 87
  George, Gov. 1, 7
  George Rockingham 131
GIVERT, Jean 45
GOULDING, Francis R. 138
  Thomas 94
GRANT, Rev. Mr. -- 31
GRANTLAND, Ann 137
GRAY, John Hannah 131
GRAYSON, W. J. 3, 5, 50, 125
GREENE, Nathanael 16
GRESHAM, -- 102
GRIER, Isaac 131
  Isaac, Rev. 19
GWINNETT, Button 27
HALL, Dr. 17, 18, 69

HALL (cont.)
  Mr. 32
  James, Rev. 16
  Lyman 27
HAMILTON, -- 110
  Alexander 69
HANNAHAN, Mr. -- 89
HARALSON, Hugh Anderson 138
HARPER, William H. 125
HARRIS, Mr. -- 93
  John, Rev. 11, 41
  Sampson Willis 136
  William L. 138
HAYNES, -- 110
HENRY, Patrick 23
HEWAT, Dr. -- 16
  Alexander, Rev. 15
HILL, Major -- 94
HILLHOUSE, Harriet Gibert 132
  Joseph 132
HILLYER, Junius 138
HOLLECK, Dr. -- 100
HOLT, Hines 138
HOUSTON, Squire 97
HULL, A. L. 139
HUMPHREYS, David 132
HUNTER, Dr. -- 71, 73
  Mr. -- 72
  John S. 132
  Squire 116
HUTCHINSON, Miss -- 104
  Abigail 103
JACKSON, Stonewall 1
JENKINS, Charles Jones 8, 126, 132
JOHNSON, Cary 23
JOHNSTON, Joseph E., Gen. 138
JONES, Charles C., Rev. 114
  George 53
  George, Dr. 132
  Noble Wymberly, II 132
  Sarah Campbell 133
  William E. 138
  Wimberley 3
KING, John Mr. 102
KNOWLTON, D. C. 130
KNOX, John 10, 11, 12, 36, 69
LACY, Drury, Rev. 25
LAMAR, John Basil 139
LANGSTON, Ruben 52
LEE, "Light Horse Harry" 23
LEGARE, -- 3, 64
  Hugh 4, 63
  Hugh S. 3
  Hugh Swinton 7, 8, 50, 63, 70, 133
  Mary 63
  Solomon 63
  Thomas 27, 28, 31, 133
LEYBURN, -- 59
  James G. 10
LINCOLN, -- 134
LOCKE, John 38
LONGSTREET, -- 52, 55, 57, 62, 65, 66
  A. B. 2, 3, 8, 45, 49, 52, 53, 81
  Augustus 34
  Augustus Baldwin 133
LONGWORTH, -- 57
LUMPKIN, John H. 139
MACLEAN, Mr. -- 72, 73

MADISON, James 23
MANN, Horace 114
MARTIN, Elizabeth 30
  William Dobbins 133
MATHER, Cotten 91
MATHIS, Robert Neil 128
MAXCY, Jonathan 70
MAYO, A. D. 61
MC DERMOT, -- 57
MC DUFFIE, -- 55, 56, 57,
  58, 110, 140
  Governor -- 92
  George 3, 4, 56, 57,
    61, 62, 70, 133
MC KOWN, Mr. -- 16
MEEK, Alexander Beaufort
  139
MEIGS, -- 107
MERIWETHER, James A. 139
MILES, James Warley 133
  William Porcher 134
MITCHELL, William Letcher
  139
MITTEN, William 133
MONROE, President -- 81
MORAGNE, Mary 65, 99, 119
  Pierre 42
MORROW, Sarah 15
MORTON, Augustus Hawkins
  134
MUNROE, President -- 35
  James 35, 79
MURRAY, Dr. -- 72
  Jacobite 15
NEWTON, Mrs. -- 111
  Elizur Lawrance 139
  John, Rev. 131
NISBET, Eugenius Aristides
  139
NOBLE, Patrick 134
  Patrick, Governor 6, 7
NORWOOD, James Alexander
  140
PALMER, Edward Gendron
  134
PATTERSON, James Cowan 134
PEERY, Benjamin F. 110
PETIGRU, -- 52, 64
  James 52
  James Lewis 2, 3, 4,
    8, 45, 52, 70, 125,
    127, 135
PICKENS, -- 140
  Andrew, General 37
  Francis W. 7, 125
  Francis Wilkinson 140
PIERCE, Franklin 127
  George Foster 140
PINNEY, Mr. -- 114
  John 140
PLEASANTS, Elizabeth 37,
  38, 111
POSEY, Mr. -- 71
  John 52, 74
  John B. 74
PRESTON, -- 110
PROVOST, General -- 127
RAMSAY, -- 64
  Dr. -- 90
  David 52
RICHARDSON, John Peter
  135
ROCHE, Maria 45
SAFFOLD, Reuben 140
SAFFORD, Joseph 140
  Joseph P. 140
SCOTT, Thomas Fielding
  140
SCREVAN, James Proctor
  135
SCREVEN, James P. 7
  James Proctor, Dr. 6

SHIELDS, Benjamin Glover
  140
SIMKINS, Eldred 89, 135,
  140
SIMMONS, Albert 82
SLATER, John F. 130
SMELT, Miss -- 104
  Mrs. -- 104
  Abigail 104
  Caroline 104, 105, 107
  Caroline Elizabeth 1
  Cornelia 105
  Dennis 104
SMITH, Dr. -- 55, 73
  President -- 24
  John Blair 23, 24
  Samuel S., Rev. Dr. 71
  Samuel Stanhope 23
SNOWDEN, Yates 106
SPEAR, William 93
SPRINGER, John, Rev. 22,
  41
STARKE, Col. -- 57, 60
STEPHENS, Alexander 8, 94,
  141
  Alexander Hamilton 88,
    140
  Linton 141
STONEY, Peter Gaillard 140
SUMNER, -- 128
  Charles 128
TAYLOR, -- 3
  John 98
  Thomas, Col. 44, 92
TELFAIR, -- 3
  Mr. -- 53
  Edward, Gov. 135
  Thomas 135
TENNENT, Gilbert 32
  William, Rev. 101
THOMPSON, Mr. -- 71, 72
  Professor -- 52
THOREAU, -- 98
THORNWELL, James H. 58
TINSLEY, James 53
TOOMBS, Robert 37, 129,
  141
WADDEL, -- 4-8, 16, 19,
  20, 24, 25, 28-37,
  40-42, 47-55, 58,
  59, 61, 63, 65-68,
  71, 72, 75, 77-80,
  82, 83, 85-88, 91-
  95, 97-118, 121,
  123, 125, 132, 137,
  139, 141
  Dr. -- 1-5, 7-9, 13,
    14, 43, 45, 46, 56-
    58, 60, 68, 71, 74,
    76, 84-88, 91, 94,
    95, 100, 111, 116,
    118-120, 122, 123,
    125, 126, 128, 132,
  Mr. -- 91
  Catherine 36, 38, 39
  Catherine Calhoun 119
  Eliza 39, 111, 112,
    117, 119
  Eliza Pleasants 111,
    112
  Elizabeth 39, 40
  Elizabeth Pleasants
    111, 112
  George 7
  Isaac 118
  Isaac Watts 39, 141
  James 125
  James, Rev. 22, 25, 26
  James Daniel 141
  James Pleasants 39,
    114, 115, 141
  John 111, 112, 113,

WADDEL, John (cont.) 125
  John Newton 39, 111,
    112, 114, 132, 141
  John W., Dr. 71
  Mary Anna 39
  Moses 1, 4, 10, 12, 13,
    14, 16-22, 25, 27,
    32, 35-39, 44, 53,
    66, 69, 70, 81, 111,
    112, 113, 117, 118,
    123, 125, 132, 139,
    141
  Moses, Jr. 39, 119
  Sarah 15, 19
  William 15, 16, 19, 28
  William Henry 141
  William Woodson 39, 141
WALKER, John 45, 100
  John William 135
WARDLAW, D. L. 136
  David Lewis 136
  Francis Hugh 136
WATTS, Isaac 102, 103
WELLBORN, Marshall
  Johnson 141
WELLS, Mr. -- 112
WHITEFIELD, -- 29
  George 28
WHITMAN, Walt 6
WILSON, Mr. -- 101
  John S. 136
WIRT, William 22
WITHERSPOON, John 17
WRIGHT, Augustus Romaldus
  141
---, Ben 91
  Dick 111
  John 48
  Old Jim 12
  Sam 2

www.ingramcontent.com/pod-product-compliance
Lightning Source LLC
Chambersburg PA
CBHW020650300426
44112CB00007B/323